The McKinsey Global Institute

The McKinsey Global Institute (MGI), established in 1990, is McKinsey & Company's business and economics research arm.

MGI's mission is to help leaders in the commercial, public, and social sectors develop a deeper understanding of the evolution of the global economy and to provide a fact base that contributes to decision making on critical management and policy issues.

MGI research combines two disciplines: economics and management. Economists often have limited access to the practical problems facing senior managers, while senior managers often lack the time and incentive to look beyond their own industry to the larger issues of the global economy. By integrating these perspectives, MGI is able to gain insights into the microeconomic underpinnings of the long-term macroeconomic trends affecting business strategy and policy making. For nearly two decades, MGI has utilized this "micro-to-macro" approach in research covering more than 20 countries and 30 industry sectors.

MGI's current research agenda focuses on three broad areas: productivity, competitiveness, and growth; the evolution of global financial markets; and the economic impact of technology. Recent research has examined a program of reform to bolster growth and renewal in Europe and the United States through accelerated productivity growth; Africa's economic potential; debt and deleveraging and the end of cheap capital; the impact of multinational companies on the US economy; technology-enabled business trends; urbanization in India and China; and the competitiveness of sectors and industrial policy.

MGI is led by three McKinsey & Company directors: Richard Dobbs, James Manyika, and Charles Roxburgh. Susan Lund serves as MGI's director of research. MGI project teams are led by a group of senior fellows and include consultants from McKinsey's offices around the world. These teams draw on McKinsey's global network of industry and management experts and partners. In addition, MGI works with leading economists, including Nobel laureates, who act as advisers to MGI projects.

The partners of McKinsey & Company fund MGI's research, which is not commissioned by any business, government, or other institution.

Further information about MGI and copies of MGI's published reports can be found at www.mckinsey.com/mgi.

McKinsey Global Institute

May 2011

Big data: The next frontier for innovation, competition, and productivity

James Manyika
Michael Chui
Brad Brown
Jacques Bughin
Richard Dobbs
Charles Roxburgh
Angela Hung Byers

Preface

The amount of data in our world has been exploding. Companies capture trillions of bytes of information about their customers, suppliers, and operations, and millions of networked sensors are being embedded in the physical world in devices such as mobile phones and automobiles, sensing, creating, and communicating data. Multimedia and individuals with smartphones and on social network sites will continue to fuel exponential growth. Big data—large pools of data that can be captured, communicated, aggregated, stored, and analyzed—is now part of every sector and function of the global economy. Like other essential factors of production such as hard assets and human capital, it is increasingly the case that much of modern economic activity, innovation, and growth simply couldn't take place without data.

The question is what this phenomenon means. Is the proliferation of data simply evidence of an increasingly intrusive world? Or can big data play a useful economic role? While most research into big data thus far has focused on the question of its volume, our study makes the case that the business and economic possibilities of big data and its wider implications are important issues that business leaders and policy makers must tackle. To inform the debate, this study examines the potential value that big data can create for organizations and sectors of the economy and seeks to illustrate and quantify that value. We also explore what leaders of organizations and policy makers need to do to capture it.

James Manyika and Michael Chui led this project, working closely with Brad Brown, Jacques Bughin, and Richard Dobbs. Charles Roxburgh also made a valuable contribution. Angela Hung Byers managed the project team, which comprised Markus Allesch, Alex Ince-Cushman, Hans Henrik Knudsen, Soyoko Umeno, and JiaJing Wang. Martin N. Baily, a senior adviser to McKinsey and a senior fellow at the Brookings Institution, and Hal R. Varian, emeritus professor in the School of Information, the Haas School of Business and the Department of Economics at the University of California at Berkeley, and chief economist at Google, served as academic advisers to this work. We are also grateful for the input provided by Erik Brynjolfsson, Schussel Family Professor at the MIT Sloan School of Management and director of the MIT Center for Digital Business, and Andrew McAfee, principal research scientist at the MIT Center for Digital Business.

The team also appreciates the contribution made by our academic research collaboration with the Global Information Industry Center (GIIC) at the University of California, San Diego, which aimed to reach a better understanding of data generation in health care and the public sector, as well as in the area of personal location data. We are grateful to Roger E. Bohn, professor of management and director at the GIIC, and James E. Short, the Center's research director, the principal investigators, as well as to graduate students Coralie Bordes, Kylie Canaday, and John Petrequin.

We are grateful for the vital input and support of numerous MGI and McKinsey colleagues including senior expert Thomas Herbig; Simon London, McKinsey director of digital communications; MGI senior fellow Jaana Remes; and expert principals William Forrest and Roger Roberts. From McKinsey's health care practice, we would like to thank Stefan Biesdorf, Basel Kayyali, Bob Kocher, Paul Mango, Sam Marwaha, Brian Milch, David Nuzum, Vivian Riefberg, Saum Sutaria, Steve Savas, and Steve Van Kuiken. From the public sector practice, we would like to acknowledge the input of Kalle Bengtsson, David Chinn, MGI fellow Karen Croxson, Thomas Dohrmann, Tim Kelsey, Alastair Levy, Lenny Mendonca, Sebastian Muschter, and Gary Pinshaw. From the retail practice, we are grateful to MGI Economics Research knowledge specialists Imran Ahmed, David Court, Karel Dörner, and John Livingston. From the manufacturing practice, we would like to thank André Andonian, Markus Löffler, Daniel Pacthod, Asutosh Padhi, Matt Rogers, and Gernot Strube. On the topic of personal location data, we would like to acknowledge the help we received from Kalle Greven, Marc de Jong, Rebecca Millman, Julian Mills, and Stephan Zimmermann. We would like to thank Martha Laboissiere for her help on our analysis of talent and Anoop Sinha and Siddhartha S for their help on mapping big data. The team also drew on previous MGI research, as well as other McKinsey research including global iConsumer surveys, *McKinsey Quarterly* Web 2.0 surveys, health care system and hospital performance benchmarking, multicountry tax benchmarking, public sector productivity, and research for the Internet Advertising Board of Europe. The team appreciates the contributions of Janet Bush, MGI senior editor, who provided editorial support; Rebeca Robboy, MGI external communications manager; Charles Barthold, external communications manager in McKinsey's Business Technology Office; Julie Philpot, MGI editorial production manager; and graphic design specialists Therese Khoury, Marisa Carder, and Bill Carlson.

This report contributes to MGI's mission to help global leaders understand the forces transforming the global economy, improve company performance, and work for better national and international policies. As with all MGI research, we would like to emphasize that this work is independent and has not been commissioned or sponsored in any way by any business, government, or other institution.

Richard Dobbs
Director, McKinsey Global Institute
Seoul

James Manyika
Director, McKinsey Global Institute
San Francisco

Charles Roxburgh
Director, McKinsey Global Institute
London

Susan Lund
Director of Research, McKinsey Global Institute
Washington, DC

June 2011

Big data—a growing torrent

$600 to buy a disk drive that can store all of the world's music

5 billion mobile phones in use in 2010

30 billion pieces of content shared on Facebook every month

40% projected growth in global data generated per year vs. **5%** growth in global IT spending

235 terabytes data collected by the US Library of Congress by April 2011

15 out of 17 sectors in the United States have more data stored per company than the US Library of Congress

Big data—capturing its value

$300 billion
potential annual value to US health care—more than double the total annual health care spending in Spain

€250 billion
potential annual value to Europe's public sector administration—more than GDP of Greece

$600 billion
potential annual consumer surplus from using personal location data globally

60%
potential increase in retailers' operating margins possible with big data

140,000–190,000
more deep analytical talent positions, and

1.5 million
more data-savvy managers needed to take full advantage of big data in the United States

Contents

Executive summary

Data have become a torrent flowing into every area of the global economy.[1] Companies churn out a burgeoning volume of transactional data, capturing trillions of bytes of information about their customers, suppliers, and operations. millions of networked sensors are being embedded in the physical world in devices such as mobile phones, smart energy meters, automobiles, and industrial machines that sense, create, and communicate data in the age of the Internet of Things.[2] Indeed, as companies and organizations go about their business and interact with individuals, they are generating a tremendous amount of digital "exhaust data," i.e., data that are created as a by-product of other activities. Social media sites, smartphones, and other consumer devices including PCs and laptops have allowed billions of individuals around the world to contribute to the amount of big data available. And the growing volume of multimedia content has played a major role in the exponential growth in the amount of big data (see Box 1, "What do we mean by 'big data'?"). Each second of high-definition video, for example, generates more than 2,000 times as many bytes as required to store a single page of text. In a digitized world, consumers going about their day—communicating, browsing, buying, sharing, searching—create their own enormous trails of data.

Box 1. What do we mean by "big data"?

"Big data" refers to datasets whose size is beyond the ability of typical database software tools to capture, store, manage, and analyze. This definition is intentionally subjective and incorporates a moving definition of how big a dataset needs to be in order to be considered big data—i.e., we don't define big data in terms of being larger than a certain number of terabytes (thousands of gigabytes). We assume that, as technology advances over time, the size of datasets that qualify as big data will also increase. Also note that the definition can vary by sector, depending on what kinds of software tools are commonly available and what sizes of datasets are common in a particular industry. With those caveats, big data in many sectors today will range from a few dozen terabytes to multiple petabytes (thousands of terabytes).

In itself, the sheer volume of data is a global phenomenon   but what does it mean? Many citizens around the world regard this collection of information with deep suspicion, seeing the data flood as nothing more than an intrusion of their privacy. But there is strong evidence that big data can play a significant economic role to the benefit not only of private commerce but also of national economies and their citizens. Our research finds that data can create significant value for the world economy, enhancing the productivity and competitiveness of companies and the

---

1   See "A special report on managing information: Data, data everywhere," *The Economist*, February 25, 2010; and special issue on "Dealing with data," *Science*, February 11, 2011.

2   "Internet of Things" refers to sensors and actuators embedded in physical objects, connected by networks to computers. See Michael Chui, Markus Löffler, and Roger Roberts, "The Internet of Things," *McKinsey Quarterly*, March 2010.

public sector and creating substantial economic surplus for consumers. For instance, if US health care could use big data creatively and effectively to drive efficiency and quality, we estimate that the potential value from data in the sector could be more than $300 billion in value every year, two-thirds of which would be in the form of reducing national health care expenditures by about 8 percent. In the private sector, we estimate, for example, that a retailer using big data to the full has the potential to increase its operating margin by more than 60 percent. In the developed economies of Europe, we estimate that government administration could save more than €100 billion ($149 billion) in operational efficiency improvements alone by using big data. This estimate does not include big data levers that could reduce fraud, errors, and tax gaps (i.e., the gap between potential and actual tax revenue).

Digital data is now everywhere—in every sector, in every economy, in every organization and user of digital technology. While this topic might once have concerned only a few data geeks, big data is now relevant for leaders across every sector, and consumers of products and services stand to benefit from its application. The ability to store, aggregate, and combine data and then use the results to perform deep analyses has become ever more accessible as trends such as Moore's Law in computing, its equivalent in digital storage, and cloud computing continue to lower costs and other technology barriers.[3] For less than $600, an individual can purchase a disk drive with the capacity to store all of the world's music.[4] The means to extract insight from data are also markedly improving as software available to apply increasingly sophisticated techniques combines with growing computing horsepower. Further, the ability to generate, communicate, share, and access data has been revolutionized by the increasing number of people, devices, and sensors that are now connected by digital networks. In 2010, more than 4 billion people, or 60 percent of the world's population, were using mobile phones, and about 12 percent of those people had smartphones, whose penetration is growing at more than 20 percent a year. More than 30 million networked sensor nodes are now present in the transportation, automotive, industrial, utilities, and retail sectors. The number of these sensors is increasing at a rate of more than 30 percent a year.

There are many ways that big data can be used to create value across sectors of the global economy. Indeed, our research suggests that we are on the cusp of a tremendous wave of innovation, productivity, and growth, as well as new modes of competition and value capture—all driven by big data as consumers, companies, and economic sectors exploit its potential. But why should this be the case now? Haven't data always been part of the impact of information and communication technology? Yes, but our research suggests that the scale and scope of changes that big data are bringing about are at an inflection point, set to expand greatly, as a series of technology trends accelerate and converge. We are already seeing visible changes in the economic landscape as a result of this convergence.

Many pioneering companies are already using big data to create value, and others need to explore how they can do the same if they are to compete. Governments, too, have a significant opportunity to boost their efficiency and the value for money

---

3   Moore's Law, first described by Intel cofounder Gordon Moore, states that the number of transistors that can be placed on an integrated circuit doubles approximately every two years. In other words, the amount of computing power that can be purchased for the same amount of money doubles about every two years. Cloud computing refers to the ability to access highly scalable computing resources through the Internet, often at lower prices than those required to install on one's own computers because the resources are shared across many users.

4   Kevin Kelly, Web 2.0 Expo and Conference, March 29, 2011. Video available at: www.web2expo.com/webexsf2011/public/schedule/proceedings.

they offer citizens at a time when public finances are constrained—and are likely to remain so due to aging populations in many countries around the world. Our research suggests that the public sector can boost its productivity significantly through the effective use of big data.

However, companies and other organizations and policy makers need to address considerable challenges if they are to capture the full potential of big data. A shortage of the analytical and managerial talent necessary to make the most of big data is a significant and pressing challenge and one that companies and policy makers can begin to address in the near term. The United States alone faces a shortage of 140,000 to 190,000 people with deep analytical skills as well as 1.5 million managers and analysts to analyze big data and make decisions based on their findings. The shortage of talent is just the beginning. Other challenges we explore in this report include the need to ensure that the right infrastructure is in place and that incentives and competition are in place to encourage continued innovation; that the economic benefits to users, organizations, and the economy are properly understood; and that safeguards are in place to address public concerns about big data.

This report seeks to understand the state of digital data, how different domains can use large datasets to create value, the potential value across stakeholders, and the implications for the leaders of private sector companies and public sector organizations, as well as for policy makers. We have supplemented our analysis of big data as a whole with a detailed examination of five domains (health care in the United States, the public sector in Europe, retail in the United States, and manufacturing and personal location data globally). This research by no means represents the final word on big data; instead, we see it as a beginning. We fully anticipate that this is a story that will continue to evolve as technologies and techniques using big data develop and data, their uses, and their economic benefits grow (alongside associated challenges and risks). For now, however, our research yields seven key insights:

1. DATA HAVE SWEPT INTO EVERY INDUSTRY AND BUSINESS FUNCTION AND ARE NOW AN IMPORTANT FACTOR OF PRODUCTION

Several research teams have studied the total amount of data generated, stored, and consumed in the world. Although the scope of their estimates and therefore their results vary, all point to exponential growth in the years ahead.[5] MGI estimates that enterprises globally stored more than 7 exabytes of new data on disk drives in 2010, while consumers stored more than 6 exabytes of new data on devices such as PCs and notebooks. One exabyte of data is the equivalent of more than 4,000 times the information stored in the US Library of Congress.[6] Indeed, we are generating so much

5 See Peter Lyman and Hal Varian, *How much information? 2003*, School of Information Management and Systems, University of California at Berkeley, 2003; papers from the IDC Digital Universe research project, sponsored by EMC, including *The expanding digital universe*, March 2007; *The diverse and exploding digital universe*, March 2008; *As the economy contracts, the digital universe expands*, May 2009, and *The digital universe decade—Are you ready?*, May 2010 (www.emc.com/leadership/programs/digital-universe.htm); two white papers from the University of California, San Diego, Global Information Industry Center: Roger Bohn and James Short, *How much information? 2009: Report on American consumers*, January 2010, and Roger Bohn, James Short, and Chaitanya Baru, *How much information? 2010: Report on enterprise server information*, January 2011; and Martin Hilbert and Priscila López, "The world's technological capacity to store, communicate, and compute information," *Science*, February 10, 2011.

6 According to the Library of Congress Web site, the US Library of Congress had 235 terabytes of storage in April 2011.

4

data today that it is physically impossible to store it all.[7] Health care providers, for instance, discard 90 percent of the data that they generate (e.g., almost all real-time video feeds created during surgery).

Big data has now reached every sector in the global economy. Like other essential factors of production such as hard assets and human capital, much of modern economic activity simply couldn't take place without it. We estimate that by 2009, nearly all sectors in the US economy had at least an average of 200 terabytes of stored data (twice the size of US retailer Wal-Mart's data warehouse in 1999) per company with more than 1,000 employees. Many sectors had more than 1 petabyte in mean stored data per company. In total, European organizations have about 70 percent of the storage capacity of the entire United States at almost 11 exabytes compared with more than 16 exabytes in 2010. Given that European economies are similar to each other in terms of their stage of development and thus their distribution of firms, we believe that the average company in most industries in Europe has enough capacity to store and manipulate big data. In contrast, the per capita data intensity in other regions is much lower. This suggests that, in the near term at least, the most potential to create value through the use of big data will be in the most developed economies. Looking ahead, however, there is huge potential to leverage big data in developing economies as long as the right conditions are in place. Consider, for instance, the fact that Asia is already the leading region for the generation of personal location data simply because so many mobile phones are in use there. More mobile phones—an estimated 800 million devices in 2010—are in use in China than in any other country. Further, some individual companies in developing regions could be far more advanced in their use of big data than averages might suggest. And some organizations will take advantage of the ability to store and process data remotely.

The possibilities of big data continue to evolve rapidly, driven by innovation in the underlying technologies, platforms, and analytic capabilities for handling data, as well as the evolution of behavior among its users as more and more individuals live digital lives.

2. BIG DATA CREATES VALUE IN SEVERAL WAYS

We have identified five broadly applicable ways to leverage big data that offer transformational potential to create value and have implications for how organizations will have to be designed, organized, and managed. For example, in a world in which large-scale experimentation is possible, how will corporate marketing functions and activities have to evolve? How will business processes change, and how will companies value and leverage their assets (particularly data assets)? Could a company's access to, and ability to analyze, data potentially confer more value than a brand? What existing business models are likely to be disrupted? For example, what happens to industries predicated on information asymmetry—e.g., various types of brokers—in a world of radical data transparency? How will incumbents tied to legacy business models and infrastructures compete with agile new attackers that are able to quickly process and take advantage of detailed consumer data that is rapidly becoming available, e.g., what they say in social media or what sensors report they are doing in the world? And what happens when surplus starts shifting from

7   For another comparison of data generation versus storage, see John F. Gantz, David Reinsel, Christopher Chute, Wolfgang Schlichting, John McArthur, Stephen Minton, Irida Xheneti, Anna Toncheva, and Alex Manfredi, "The expanding digital universe," IDC white paper, sponsored by EMC, March 2007.

suppliers to customers, as they become empowered by their own access to data, e.g., comparisons of prices and quality across competitors?

Creating transparency

Simply making big data more easily accessible to relevant stakeholders in a timely manner can create tremendous value. In the public sector, for example, making relevant data more readily accessible across otherwise separated departments can sharply reduce search and processing time. In manufacturing, integrating data from R&D, engineering, and manufacturing units to enable concurrent engineering can significantly cut time to market and improve quality.

Enabling experimentation to discover needs, expose variability, and improve performance

As they create and store more transactional data in digital form, organizations can collect more accurate and detailed performance data (in real or near real time) on everything from product inventories to personnel sick days. IT enables organizations to instrument processes and then set up controlled experiments. Using data to analyze variability in performance—that which either occurs naturally or is generated by controlled experiments—and to understand its root causes can enable leaders to manage performance to higher levels.

Segmenting populations to customize actions

Big data allows organizations to create highly specific segmentations and to tailor products and services precisely to meet those needs. This approach is well known in marketing and risk management but can be revolutionary elsewhere—for example, in the public sector where an ethos of treating all citizens in the same way is commonplace. Even consumer goods and service companies that have used segmentation for many years are beginning to deploy ever more sophisticated big data techniques such as the real-time microsegmentation of customers to target promotions and advertising.

Replacing/supporting human decision making with automated algorithms

Sophisticated analytics can substantially improve decision making, minimize risks, and unearth valuable insights that would otherwise remain hidden. Such analytics have applications for organizations from tax agencies that can use automated risk engines to flag candidates for further examination to retailers that can use algorithms to optimize decision processes such as the automatic fine-tuning of inventories and pricing in response to real-time in-store and online sales. In some cases, decisions will not necessarily be automated but augmented by analyzing huge, entire datasets using big data techniques and technologies rather than just smaller samples that individuals with spreadsheets can handle and understand. Decision making may never be the same; some organizations are already making better decisions by analyzing entire datasets from customers, employees, or even sensors embedded in products.

Innovating new business models, products, and services

Big data enables companies to create new products and services, enhance existing ones, and invent entirely new business models. Manufacturers are using data obtained from the use of actual products to improve the development of the next generation of products and to create innovative after-sales service offerings. The emergence of real-time location data has created an entirely new set of location-based services from navigation to pricing property and casualty insurance based on where, and how, people drive their cars.

3. USE OF BIG DATA WILL BECOME A KEY BASIS OF COMPETITION AND GROWTH FOR INDIVIDUAL FIRMS

The use of big data is becoming a key way for leading companies to outperform their peers. For example, we estimate that a retailer embracing big data has the potential to increase its operating margin by more than 60 percent. We have seen leading retailers such as the United Kingdom's Tesco use big data to capture market share from its local competitors, and many other examples abound in industries such as financial services and insurance. Across sectors, we expect to see value accruing to leading users of big data at the expense of laggards, a trend for which the emerging evidence is growing stronger.[8] Forward-thinking leaders can begin to aggressively build their organizations' big data capabilities. This effort will take time, but the impact of developing a superior capacity to take advantage of big data will confer enhanced competitive advantage over the long term and is therefore well worth the investment to create this capability. But the converse is also true. In a big data world, a competitor that fails to sufficiently develop its capabilities will be left behind.

Big data will also help to create new growth opportunities and entirely new categories of companies, such as those that aggregate and analyze industry data. Many of these will be companies that sit in the middle of large information flows where data about products and services, buyers and suppliers, and consumer preferences and intent can be captured and analyzed. Examples are likely to include companies that interface with large numbers of consumers buying a wide range of products and services, companies enabling global supply chains, companies that process millions of transactions, and those that provide platforms for consumer digital experiences. These will be the big-data-advantaged businesses. More businesses will find themselves with some kind of big data advantage than one might at first think. Many companies have access to valuable pools of data generated by their products and services. Networks will even connect physical products, enabling those products to report their own serial numbers, ship dates, number of times used, and so on.

Some of these opportunities will generate new sources of value; others will cause major shifts in value within industries. For example, medical clinical information providers, which aggregate data and perform the analyses necessary to improve health care efficiency, could compete in a market worth more than $10 billion by 2020. Early movers that secure access to the data necessary to create value are likely to reap the most benefit (see Box 2, "How do we measure the value of big data?"). From the standpoint of competitiveness and the potential capture of value, all companies need to take big data seriously. In most industries, established competitors and new entrants alike will leverage data-driven strategies to innovate, compete, and capture value. Indeed, we found early examples of such use of data in every sector we examined.

---

8   Erik Brynjolfsson, Lorin M. Hitt, and Heekyung Hellen Kim, Strength in numbers: *How does data-driven decisionmaking affect firm performance?*, April 22, 2011, available at SSRN (ssrn. com/abstract=1819486).

Box 2. How do we measure the value of big data?

When we set out to size the potential of big data to create value, we considered only those actions that essentially depend on the use of big data—i.e., actions where the use of big data is necessary (but usually not sufficient) to execute a particular lever. We did not include the value of levers that consist only of automation but do not involve big data (e.g., productivity increases from replacing bank tellers with ATMs). Note also that we include the gross value of levers that require the use of big data. We did not attempt to estimate big data's relative contribution to the value generated by a particular lever but rather estimated the total value created.

4. THE USE OF BIG DATA WILL UNDERPIN NEW WAVES OF PRODUCTIVITY GROWTH AND CONSUMER SURPLUS

Across the five domains we studied, we identified many big data levers that will, in our view, underpin substantial productivity growth (Exhibit 1). These opportunities have the potential to improve efficiency and effectiveness, enabling organizations both to do more with less and to produce higher-quality outputs, i.e., increase the value-added content of products and services.[9] For example, we found that companies can leverage data to design products that better match customer needs. Data can even be leveraged to improve products as they are used. An example is a mobile phone that has learned its owner's habits and preferences, that holds applications and data tailored to that particular user's needs, and that will therefore be more valuable than a new device that is not customized to a user's needs.[10] Capturing this potential requires innovation in operations and processes. Examples include augmenting decision making—from clinical practice to tax audits—with algorithms as well as making innovations in products and services, such as accelerating the development of new drugs by using advanced analytics and creating new, proactive after-sales maintenance service for automobiles through the use of networked sensors. Policy makers who understand that accelerating productivity within sectors is the key lever for increasing the standard of living in their economies as a whole need to ease the way for organizations to take advantage of big data levers that enhance productivity.

We also find a general pattern in which customers, consumers, and citizens capture a large amount of the economic surplus that big data enables—they are both direct and indirect beneficiaries of big-data-related innovation.[11] For example, the use of big data can enable improved health outcomes, higher-quality civic engagement with government, lower prices due to price transparency, and a better match between products and consumer needs. We expect this trend toward enhanced consumer surplus to continue and accelerate across all sectors as they deploy big data. Take the area of personal location data as illustration. In this area, the use of real-time traffic information to inform navigation will create a quantifiable consumer surplus through

---

9   Note that the effectiveness improvement is not captured in some of the productivity calculations because of a lack of precision in some metrics such as improved health outcomes or better matching the needs of consumers with goods in retail services. Thus, in many cases, our productivity estimates are likely to be conservative.

10 Hal Varian has described the ability of products to leverage data to improve with use as "product kaizen." See Hal Varian, *Computer mediated transactions*, 2010 Ely Lecture at the American Economics Association meeting, Atlanta, Georgia.

11 Professor Erik Brynjolfsson of the Massachusetts Institute of Technology has noted that the creation of large amounts of consumer surplus, not captured in traditional economic metrics such as GDP, is a characteristic of the deployment of IT.

savings on the time spent traveling and on fuel consumption. Mobile location-enabled applications will create surplus from consumers, too. In both cases, the surplus these innovations create is likely to far exceed the revenue generated by service providers. For consumers to benefit, policy makers will often need to push the deployment of big data innovations.

Exhibit 1

Big data can generate significant financial value across sectors

US health care
- $300 billion value per year
- ~0.7 percent annual productivity growth

Europe public sector administration
- €250 billion value per year
- ~0.5 percent annual productivity growth

Global personal location data
- $100 billion+ revenue for service providers
- Up to $700 billion value to end users

US retail
- 60+% increase in net margin possible
- 0.5–1.0 percent annual productivity growth

Manufacturing
- Up to 50 percent decrease in product development, assembly costs
- Up to 7 percent reduction in working capital

SOURCE: McKinsey Global Institute analysis

5. WHILE THE USE OF BIG DATA WILL MATTER ACROSS SECTORS, SOME SECTORS ARE POISED FOR GREATER GAINS

Illustrating differences among different sectors, if we compare the historical productivity of sectors in the United States with the potential of these sectors to capture value from big data (using an index that combines several quantitative metrics), we observe that patterns vary from sector to sector (Exhibit 2).[12]

---

12 The index consists of five metrics that are designed as proxies to indicate (1) the amount of data available for use and analysis; (2) variability in performance; (3) number of stakeholders (customers and suppliers) with which an organization deals on average; (4) transaction intensity; and (5) turbulence inherent in a sector. We believe that these are the characteristics that make a sector more or less likely to take advantage of the five transformative big data opportunities. See the appendix for further details.

Exhibit 2

Some sectors are positioned for greater gains from the use of big data

Historical productivity growth in the United States, 2000–08

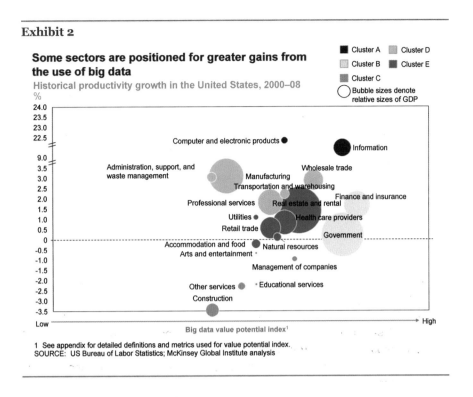

1 See appendix for detailed definitions and metrics used for value potential index.
SOURCE: US Bureau of Labor Statistics; McKinsey Global Institute analysis

Computer and electronic products and information sectors (Cluster A), traded globally, stand out as sectors that have already been experiencing very strong productivity growth and that are poised to gain substantially from the use of big data. Two services sectors (Cluster B)—finance and insurance and government—are positioned to benefit very strongly from big data as long as barriers to its use can be overcome. Several sectors (Cluster C) have experienced negative productivity growth, probably indicating that these sectors face strong systemic barriers to increasing productivity. Among the remaining sectors, we see that globally traded sectors (mostly Cluster D) tend to have experienced higher historical productivity growth, while local services (mainly Cluster E) have experienced lower growth.

While all sectors will have to overcome barriers to capture value from the use of big data, barriers are structurally higher for some than for others (Exhibit 3). For example, the public sector, including education, faces higher hurdles because of a lack of data-driven mind-set and available data. Capturing value in health care faces challenges given the relatively low IT investment performed so far. Sectors such as retail, manufacturing, and professional services may have relatively lower degrees of barriers to overcome for precisely the opposite reasons.

Exhibit 3

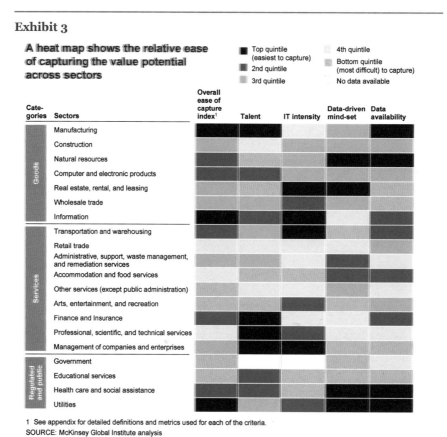

A heat map shows the relative ease of capturing the value potential across sectors

Legend:
- ■ Top quintile (easiest to capture)
- ■ 2nd quintile
- ■ 3rd quintile
- □ 4th quintile
- ▨ Bottom quintile (most difficult) to capture)
- No data available

Categories	Sectors	Overall ease of capture index[1]	Talent	IT intensity	Data-driven mind-set	Data availability
Goods	Manufacturing					
	Construction					
	Natural resources					
	Computer and electronic products					
	Real estate, rental, and leasing					
	Wholesale trade					
	Information					
Services	Transportation and warehousing					
	Retail trade					
	Administrative, support, waste management, and remediation services					
	Accommodation and food services					
	Other services (except public administration)					
	Arts, entertainment, and recreation					
	Finance and Insurance					
	Professional, scientific, and technical services					
	Management of companies and enterprises					
Regulated and public	Government					
	Educational services					
	Health care and social assistance					
	Utilities					

1 See appendix for detailed definitions and metrics used for each of the criteria.
SOURCE: McKinsey Global Institute analysis

6. THERE WILL BE A SHORTAGE OF TALENT NECESSARY FOR ORGANIZATIONS TO TAKE ADVANTAGE OF BIG DATA

A significant constraint on realizing value from big data will be a shortage of talent, particularly of people with deep expertise in statistics and machine learning, and the managers and analysts who know how to operate companies by using insights from big data.

In the United States, we expect big data to rapidly become a key determinant of competition across sectors. But we project that demand for deep analytical positions in a big data world could exceed the supply being produced on current trends by 140,000 to 190,000 positions (Exhibit 4). Furthermore, this type of talent is difficult to produce, taking years of training in the case of someone with intrinsic mathematical abilities. Although our quantitative analysis uses the United States as illustration, we believe that the constraint on this type of talent will be global, with the caveat that some regions may be able to produce the supply that can fill talent gaps in other regions.

In addition, we project a need for 1.5 million additional managers and analysts in the United States who can ask the right questions and consume the results of the analysis of big data effectively. The United States—and other economies facing similar shortages—cannot fill this gap simply by changing graduate requirements and waiting for people to graduate with more skills or by importing talent (although these could be important actions to take). It will be necessary to retrain a significant amount of the talent in place; fortunately, this level of training does not require years of dedicated study.

Exhibit 4

**Demand for deep analytical talent in the United States could be
50 to 60 percent greater than its projected supply by 2018**

Supply and demand of deep analytical talent by 2018
Thousand people

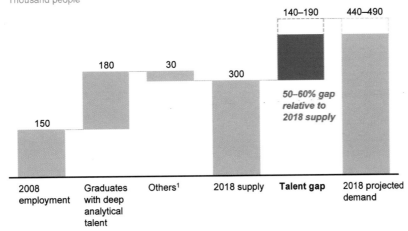

1 Other supply drivers include attrition (-), immigration (+), and reemploying previously unemployed deep analytical talent (+).
SOURCE: US Bureau of Labor Statistics; US Census; Dun & Bradstreet; company interviews; McKinsey Global Institute analysis

7. SEVERAL ISSUES WILL HAVE TO BE ADDRESSED TO CAPTURE THE FULL POTENTIAL OF BIG DATA

Data policies. As an ever larger amount of data is digitized and travels across organizational boundaries, there is a set of policy issues that will become increasingly important, including, but not limited to, privacy, security, intellectual property, and liability. Clearly, privacy is an issue whose importance, particularly to consumers, is growing as the value of big data becomes more apparent. Personal data such as health and financial records are often those that can offer the most significant human benefits, such as helping to pinpoint the right medical treatment or the most appropriate financial product. However, consumers also view these categories of data as being the most sensitive. It is clear that individuals and the societies in which they live will have to grapple with trade-offs between privacy and utility.

Another closely related concern is data security, e.g., how to protect competitively sensitive data or other data that should be kept private. Recent examples have demonstrated that data breaches can expose not only personal consumer information and confidential corporate information but even national security secrets. With serious breaches on the rise, addressing data security through technological and policy tools will become essential.[13]

Big data's increasing economic importance also raises a number of legal issues, especially when coupled with the fact that data are fundamentally different from many other assets. Data can be copied perfectly and easily combined with other data. The same piece of data can be used simultaneously by more than one person. All of these are unique characteristics of data compared with physical assets. Questions about the intellectual property rights attached to data will have to be answered: Who "owns" a piece of data and what rights come attached with a dataset? What defines "fair use" of data? There are also questions related to liability: Who is responsible when an

13 Data privacy and security are being studied and debated at great length elsewhere, so we have not made these topics the focus of the research reported here.

inaccurate piece of data leads to negative consequences? Such types of legal issues will need clarification, probably over time, to capture the full potential of big data.

Technology and techniques. To capture value from big data, organizations will have to deploy new technologies (e.g., storage, computing, and analytical software) and techniques (i.e., new types of analyses). The range of technology challenges and the priorities set for tackling them will differ depending on the data maturity of the institution. Legacy systems and incompatible standards and formats too often prevent the integration of data and the more sophisticated analytics that create value from big data. New problems and growing computing power will spur the development of new analytical techniques. There is also a need for ongoing innovation in technologies and techniques that will help individuals and organizations to integrate, analyze, visualize, and consume the growing torrent of big data.

Organizational change and talent. Organizational leaders often lack the understanding of the value in big data as well as how to unlock this value. In competitive sectors this may prove to be an Achilles heel for some companies since their established competitors as well as new entrants are likely to leverage big data to compete against them. And, as we have discussed, many organizations do not have the talent in place to derive insights from big data. In addition, many organizations today do not structure workflows and incentives in ways that optimize the use of big data to make better decisions and take more informed action.

Access to data. To enable transformative opportunities, companies will increasingly need to integrate information from multiple data sources. In some cases, organizations will be able to purchase access to the data. In other cases, however, gaining access to third-party data is often not straightforward. The sources of third-party data might not have considered sharing it. Sometimes, economic incentives are not aligned to encourage stakeholders to share data. A stakeholder that holds a certain dataset might consider it to be the source of a key competitive advantage and thus would be reluctant to share it with other stakeholders. Other stakeholders must find ways to offer compelling value propositions to holders of valuable data.

Industry structure. Sectors with a relative lack of competitive intensity and performance transparency, along with industries where profit pools are highly concentrated, are likely to be slow to fully leverage the benefits of big data. For example, in the public sector, there tends to be a lack of competitive pressure that limits efficiency and productivity; as a result, the sector faces more difficult barriers than other sectors in the way of capturing the potential value from using big data. US health care is another example of how the structure of an industry impacts on how easy it will be to extract value from big data. This is a sector that not only has a lack of performance transparency into cost and quality but also an industry structure in which payors will gain (from fewer payouts for unnecessary treatment) from the use of clinical data. However, the gains accruing to payors will be at the expense of the providers (fewer medical activities to charge for) from whom the payors would have to obtain the clinical data. As these examples suggest, organization leaders and policy makers will have to consider how industry structures could evolve in a big data world if they are to determine how to optimize value creation at the level of individual firms, sectors, and economies as a whole.

□ □ □

The effective use of big data has the potential to transform economies, delivering a new wave of productivity growth and consumer surplus. Using big data will become a key basis of competition for existing companies, and will create new competitors who are able to attract employees that have the critical skills for a big data world. Leaders of organizations need to recognize the potential opportunity as well as the strategic threats that big data represent and should assess and then close any gap between their current IT capabilities and their data strategy and what is necessary to capture big data opportunities relevant to their enterprise. They will need to be creative and proactive in determining which pools of data they can combine to create value and how to gain access to those pools, as well as addressing security and privacy issues. On the topic of privacy and security, part of the task could include helping consumers to understand what benefits the use of big data offers, along with the risks. In parallel, companies need to recruit and retain deep analytical talent and retrain their analyst and management ranks to become more data savvy, establishing a culture that values and rewards the use of big data in decision making.

Policy makers need to recognize the potential of harnessing big data to unleash the next wave of growth in their economies. They need to provide the institutional framework to allow companies to easily create value out of data while protecting the privacy of citizens and providing data security. They also have a significant role to play in helping to mitigate the shortage of talent through education and immigration policy and putting in place technology enablers including infrastructure such as communication networks; accelerating research in selected areas including advanced analytics; and creating an intellectual property framework that encourages innovation. Creative solutions to align incentives may also be necessary, including, for instance, requirements to share certain data to promote the public welfare.

1. Mapping global data: Growth and value creation

Many of the most powerful inventions throughout human history, from language to the modern computer, were those that enabled people to better generate, capture, and consume data and information.[14] We have witnessed explosive growth in the amount of data in our world. Big data has reached critical mass in every sector and function of the typical economy, and the rapid development and diffusion of digital information technologies have intensified its growth.

We estimate that new data stored by enterprises exceeded 7 exabytes of data globally in 2010 and that new data stored by consumers around the world that year exceeded an additional 6 exabytes.[15] To put these very large numbers in context, the data that companies and individuals are producing and storing is equivalent to filling more than 60,000 US Libraries of Congress. If all words spoken by humans were digitized as text, they would total about 5 exabytes—less than the new data stored by consumers in a year.[16] The increasing volume and detail of information captured by enterprises, together with the rise of multimedia, social media, and the Internet of Things will fuel exponential growth in data for the foreseeable future.

There is no doubt that the sheer size and rapidly expanding universe of big data are phenomena in themselves and have been the primary focus of research thus far. But the key question is what broader impact this torrent of data might have. Many consumers are suspicious about the amount of data that is collected about every aspect of their lives, from how they shop to how healthy they are. Is big data simply a sign of how intrusive society has become, or can big data, in fact, play a useful role in economic terms that can benefit all societal stakeholders?

The emphatic answer is that data can indeed create significant value for the world economy, potentially enhancing the productivity and competitiveness of companies and creating a substantial economic surplus for consumers and their governments. Building on MGI's deep background in analyzing productivity and competitiveness around the world, this research explores a fresh linkage between data and productivity. Although the relationship between productivity and IT investments is well established, exploring the link between productivity and data breaks new ground. Based on our findings, we believe that the global economy is on the cusp of a new wave of productivity growth enabled by big data.

In this chapter, we look at past and current research on sizing big data and its storage capacity. We then explore the likely relationship between big data and productivity, drawing on past analyses of the impact of IT investment and innovation to drive

---

14 For an interesting perspective on this topic, see James Gleick, *The information: A history. A theory. A flood* (New York, NY: Pantheon Books, 2011).

15 Our definition of new data stored describes the amount of digital storage newly taken up by data in a year. Note that this differs from Hal Varian and Peter Lyman's definition of new data stored as our methodology does not take into account data created and stored but then written over in a year. See the appendix for further details

16 Peter Lyman and Hal R. Varian, *How much information? 2003*, School of Information Management and Systems, University of California at Berkeley, 2003.

productivity that we believe is directly applicable to the current and likely future evolution of big data.

THE VOLUME OF DATA IS GROWING AT AN EXPONENTIAL RATE

MGI is the latest of several research groups to study the amount of data that enterprises and individuals are generating, storing, and consuming throughout the global economy. All analyses, each with different methodologies and definitions, agree on one fundamental point—the amount of data in the world has been expanding rapidly and will continue to grow exponentially for the foreseeable future (see Box 3, "Measuring data") despite there being a question mark over how much data we, as human beings, can absorb (see Box 4, "Human beings may have limits in their ability to consume and understand big data" on page 18).

Box 3. Measuring data

Measuring volumes of data provokes a number of methodological questions. First, how can we distinguish data from information and from insight? Common definitions describe data as being raw indicators, information as the meaningful interpretation of those signals, and insight as an actionable piece of knowledge. For the purposes of sizing big data in this research, we focused primarily on data sized in terms of bytes. But a second question then arises. When using bytes, what types of encoding should we use? In other words, what is the amount of assumed compression in the encoding? We have chosen to assume the most common encoding methods used for each type of data.

Hal Varian and Peter Lyman at the University of California Berkeley were pioneers in the research into the amount of data produced, stored, and transmitted. As part of their "How much information?" project that ran from 2000 to 2003, the authors estimated that 5 exabytes of new data were stored globally in 2002 (92 percent on magnetic media) and that more than three times that amount—18 exabytes—of new or original data were transmitted, but not necessarily stored, through electronic channels such as telephone, radio, television, and the Internet. Most important, they estimated that the amount of new data stored doubled from 1999 to 2002, a compound annual growth rate of 25 percent.

Then, starting in 2007, the information-management company EMC sponsored the research firm IDC to produce an annual series of reports on the "Digital Universe" to size the amount of digital information created and replicated each year.[17] This analysis showed that in 2007, the amount of digital data created in a year exceeded the world's data storage capacity for the first time. In short, there was no way to actually store all of the digital data being created. They also found that the rate at which data generation is increasing is much faster than the world's data storage capacity is expanding, pointing strongly to the continued widening of the gap between the two. Their analysis estimated that the total amount of data created and replicated in 2009 was 800 exabytes—enough to fill a stack of DVDs reaching to the moon and back. They projected that this volume would grow by 44 times to 2020, an implied annual growth rate of 40 percent.[18]

---

17 IDC has published a series of white papers, sponsored by EMC, including "The expanding digital universe," March 2007; "The diverse and exploding digital universe," March 2008; "As the economy contracts, the digital universe expands," May 2009; and "The digital universe decade—Are you ready?," May 2010. All are available at www.emc.com/leadership/programs/digital-universe.htm.

18 The IDC estimates of the volume of data include copies of data, not just originally generated data.

Most recently, Martin Hilbert and Priscila López published a paper in *Science* that analyzed total global storage and computing capacity from 1986 to 2007.[19] Their analysis showed that while global storage capacity grew at an annual rate of 23 percent over that period (to more than 290 exabytes in 2007 for all analog and digital media), general-purpose computing capacity, a measure of the ability to generate and process data, grew at a much higher annual rate of 58 percent. Their study also documented the rise of digitization. They estimated that the percentage of data stored in digital form increased from only 25 percent in 2000 (analog forms such as books, photos, and audio/video tapes making up the bulk of data storage capacity at that time) to a dominant 94 percent share in 2007 as media such as hard drives, CDs, and digital tapes grew in importance (Exhibits 5 and 6).

Exhibit 5

Data storage has grown significantly, shifting markedly from analog to digital after 2000

Global installed, optimally compressed, storage

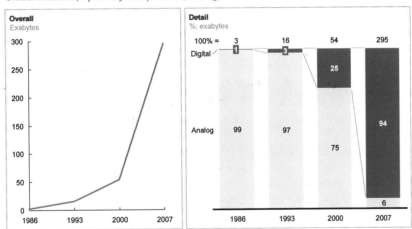

NOTE: Numbers may not sum due to rounding.
SOURCE: Hilbert and López, "The world's technological capacity to store, communicate, and compute information," *Science*, 2011

Exhibit 6

Computation capacity has also risen sharply

Global installed computation to handle information

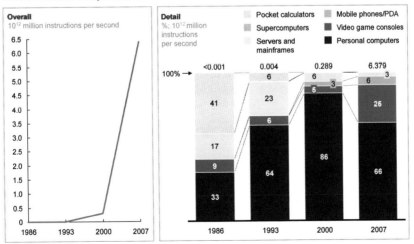

NOTE: Numbers may not sum due to rounding.
SOURCE: Hilbert and López, "The world's technological capacity to store, communicate, and compute information," *Science*, 2011

19 Martin Hilbert and Priscila López, "The world's technological capacity to store, communicate, and compute information," *Science*, February 10, 2011.

Box 4. Human beings may have limits in their ability to consume and understand big data

The generation of big data may be growing exponentially and advancing technology may allow the global economy to store and process ever greater quantities of data, but there may be limits to our innate human ability—our sensory and cognitive faculties—to process this data torrent. It is said that the mind can handle about seven pieces of information in its short-term memory.[1] Roger Bohn and James Short at the University of California at San Diego discovered that the rate of growth in data consumed by consumers, through various types of media, was a relatively modest 2.8 percent in bytes per hour between 1980 and 2008. We should note that one of the reasons for this slow growth was the relatively fixed number of bytes delivered through television before the widespread adoption of high-definition digital video.[2] The topic of information overload has been widely studied by academics from neuroscientists to economists. Economist Herbert Simon once said, "A wealth of information creates a poverty of attention and a need to allocate that attention efficiently among the overabundance of information sources that might consume it."[3]

Despite these apparent limits, there are ways to help organizations and individuals to process, visualize, and synthesize meaning from big data. For instance, more sophisticated visualization techniques and algorithms, including automated algorithms, can enable people to see patterns in large amounts of data and help them to unearth the most pertinent insights (see chapter 2 for examples of visualization). Advancing collaboration technology also allows a large number of individuals, each of whom may possess understanding of a special area of information, to come together in order to create a whole picture to tackle interdisciplinary problems. If organizations and individuals deployed such techniques more widely, end-user demand for big data could strengthen significantly.

---

1   George A. Miller, "The magical number seven, plus or minus two: Some limits on our capacity for processing information," *Psychological Review*, Volume 63(2), March 1956. 81–97.

2   Roger Bohn and James Short, *How much information? 2009: Report on American consumers*, University of California, San Diego, Global Information Industry Center, January 2010.

3   Herbert A. Simon, "Designing organizations for an information-rich world," in Martin Greenberger, *Computers, Communication, and the Public Interest*, Baltimore, MD: The Johns Hopkins Press, 1971.

THE INTENSITY OF BIG DATA VARIES ACROSS SECTORS BUT HAS REACHED CRITICAL MASS IN EVERY SECTOR

There is broad agreement that data generation has been growing exponentially. Has that growth been concentrated only in certain segments of the global economy? The answer to that question is no. The growth of big data is a phenomenon that we have observed in every sector. More important, data intensity—i.e., the average amount of data stored per company—across sectors in the global economy is sufficient for companies to use techniques enabled by large datasets to drive value (although some sectors had significantly higher data intensity than others). Business leaders across sectors are now beginning to ask themselves how they can better derive value from their data assets, but we would argue that leaders in sectors with high data intensity in particular should make examining the potential a high priority.

MGI estimates that enterprises around the world used more than 7 exabytes of incremental disk drive data storage capacity in 2010; nearly 80 percent of that total appeared to duplicate data that had been stored elsewhere.[20] We also analyzed data generation and storage at the level of sectors and individual firms. We estimate that, by 2009, nearly all sectors in the US economy had at least an average of 200 terabytes of stored data per company (for companies with more than 1,000 employees) and that many sectors had more than 1 petabyte in mean stored data per company. Some individual companies have far higher stored data than their sector average, potentially giving them more potential to capture value from big data.

Some sectors Exhibit far higher levels of data intensity than others, implying that they have more near-term potential to capture value from big data. Financial services sectors, including securities and investment services and banking, have the most digital data stored per firm on average. This probably reflects the fact that firms involved in these sectors tend to be transaction-intensive (the New York Stock Exchange, for instance, boasts about half a trillion trades a month) and that, on average, these types of sectors tend to have a preponderance of large firms. Communications and media firms, utilities, and government also have significant digital data stored per enterprise or organization, which appears to reflect the fact that such entities have a high volume of operations and multimedia data. Discrete and process manufacturing have the highest aggregate data stored in bytes. However, these sectors rank much lower in intensity terms, since they are fragmented into a large number of firms. Because individual firms often do not share data, the value they can obtain from big data could be constrained by the degree to which they can pool data across manufacturing supply chains (see chapter 3d on manufacturing for more detail) (Exhibit 7).

Exhibit 7

Companies in all sectors have at least 100 terabytes of stored data in the United States; many have more than 1 petabyte

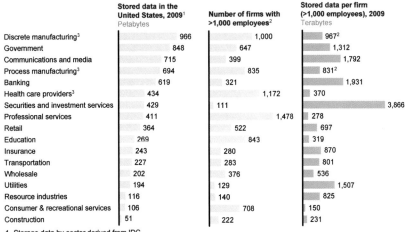

	Stored data in the United States, 2009[1] Petabytes	Number of firms with >1,000 employees[2]	Stored data per firm (>1,000 employees), 2009 Terabytes
Discrete manufacturing[3]	966	1,000	967[2]
Government	848	647	1,312
Communications and media	715	399	1,792
Process manufacturing[3]	694	835	831[2]
Banking	619	321	1,931
Health care providers[3]	434	1,172	370
Securities and investment services	429	111	3,866
Professional services	411	1,478	278
Retail	364	522	697
Education	269	843	319
Insurance	243	280	870
Transportation	227	283	801
Wholesale	202	376	536
Utilities	194	129	1,507
Resource industries	116	140	825
Consumer & recreational services	106	708	150
Construction	51	222	231

1 Storage data by sector derived from IDC.
2 Firm data split into sectors, when needed, using employment
3 The particularly large number of firms in manufacturing and health care provider sectors make the available storage per company much smaller.
SOURCE: IDC; US Bureau of Labor Statistics; McKinsey Global Institute analysis

---

20 This is an estimate of the additional capacity utilized during the year. In some cases, this capacity could consist of multiple sets of data overwriting other data, but the capacity usage is incremental over the storage capacity used the previous year.

In addition to variations in the amount of data stored in different sectors, the types of data generated and stored—i.e., whether the data encodes video, images, audio, or text/numeric information—also differ markedly from industry to industry. For instance, financial services, administrative parts of government, and retail and wholesale all generate significant amounts of text and numerical data including customer data, transaction information, and mathematical modeling and simulations (Exhibit 8). Other sectors such as manufacturing, health care, and communications and media are responsible for higher percentages of multimedia data. Manufacturing generates a great deal of text and numerical data in its production processes, but R&D and engineering functions in many manufacturing subsectors are heavy users of image data used in design.

Image data in the form of X-rays, CT, and other scans dominate data storage volumes in health care. While a single page of records can total a kilobyte, a single image can require 20 to 200 megabytes or more to store. In the communications and media industries, byte-hungry images and audio dominate storage volumes. Indeed, if we were to examine pure data generation (rather than storage), some subsectors such as health care and gaming generate even more multimedia data in the form of real-time procedure and surveillance video, respectively, but this is rarely stored for long.

Exhibit 8

The type of data generated and stored varies by sector[1]

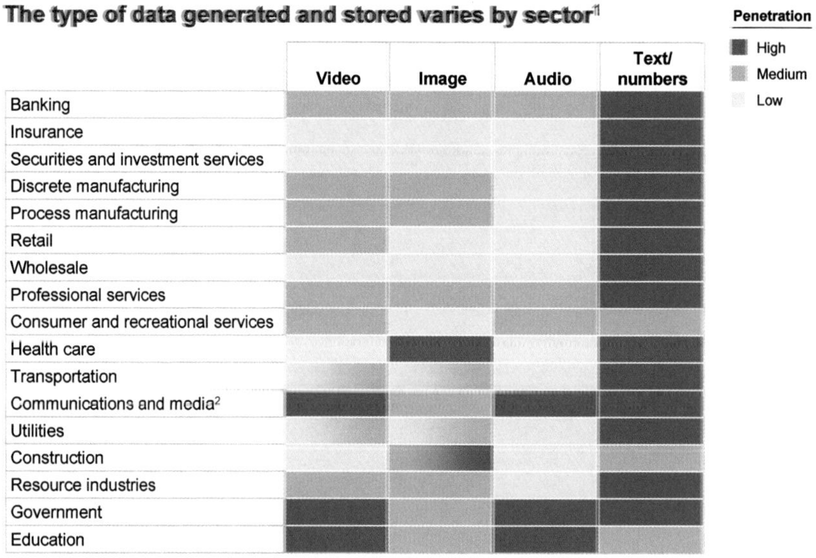

	Video	Image	Audio	Text/ numbers
Banking				
Insurance				
Securities and investment services				
Discrete manufacturing				
Process manufacturing				
Retail				
Wholesale				
Professional services				
Consumer and recreational services				
Health care				
Transportation				
Communications and media[2]				
Utilities				
Construction				
Resource industries				
Government				
Education				

Penetration
- High
- Medium
- Low

1 We compiled this heat map using units of data (in files or minutes of video) rather than bytes.
2 Video and audio are high in some subsectors.
SOURCE: McKinsey Global Institute analysis

Turning to a geographic profile of where big data are stored, North America and Europe together lead the pack with a combined 70 percent of the global total currently. However, both developed and emerging markets are expected to experience strong growth in data storage and, by extension, data generation at rates of anywhere between 35 and 45 percent a year. An effort to profile the distribution of data around the world needs to take into account that data are not always stored in the country where they are generated; data centers in one region can store and analyze data generated in another.

MAJOR ESTABLISHED TRENDS WILL CONTINUE TO DRIVE DATA GROWTH

Across sectors and regions, several cross-cutting trends have fueled growth in data generation and will continue to propel the rapidly expanding pools of data. These trends include growth in traditional transactional databases, continued expansion of multimedia content, increasing popularity of social media, and proliferation of applications of sensors in the Internet of Things.

Enterprises are collecting data with greater granularity and frequency, capturing every customer transaction, attaching more personal information, and also collecting more information about consumer behavior in many different environments. This activity simultaneously increases the need for more storage and analytical capacity. Tesco, for instance, generates more than 1.5 billion new items of data every month. Wal-Mart's warehouse now includes some 2.5 petabytes of information, the equivalent of roughly half of all the letters delivered by the US Postal Service in 2010.

The increasing use of multimedia in sectors including health care and consumer-facing industries has contributed significantly to the growth of big data and will continue to do so. Videos generate a tremendous amount of data. Every minute of the now most commonly used high-resolution video in surgeries generates 25 times the data volume (per minute) of even the highest resolution still images such as CT scans, and each of those still images already requires thousands of times more bytes than a single page of text or numerical data. More than 95 percent of the clinical data generated in health care is now video. Multimedia data already accounts for more than half of Internet backbone traffic (i.e., the traffic carried on the largest connections between major Internet networks), and this share is expected to grow to 70 percent by 2013.[21]

The surge in the use of social media is producing its own stream of new data. While social networks dominate the communications portfolios of younger users, older users are adopting them at an even more rapid pace. McKinsey surveyed users of digital services and found a 7 percent increase in 2009 in use of social networks by people aged 25 to 34, an even more impressive 21 to 22 percent increase among those aged 35 to 54, and an eye-opening 52 percent increase in usage among those aged 55 to 64. The rapid adoption of smartphones is also driving up the usage of social networking (Exhibit 9). Facebook's 600 million active users spend more than 9.3 billion hours a month on the site—if Facebook were a country, it would have the third-largest population in the world. Every month, the average Facebook user creates 90 pieces of content and the network itself shares more than 30 billion items of content including photos, notes, blog posts, Web links, and news stories. YouTube says it has some 490 million unique visitors worldwide who spend more than 2.9 billion hours on the site each month. YouTube claims to upload 24 hours of video every minute, making the site a hugely significant data aggregator. McKinsey has also documented how the use of social media and Web 2.0 has been migrating from the consumer realm into the enterprise.[22]

Increasing applications of the Internet of Things, i.e., sensors and devices embedded in the physical world and connected by networks to computing resources, is another trend driving growth in big data.[23] McKinsey research projects that the number of

---

21 IDC Internet consumer traffic analysis, 2010.

22 Michael Chui, Andy Miller, and Roger Roberts. "Six ways to make Web 2.0 work," *McKinsey Quarterly*, February 2009; Jaques Bughin and Michael Chui, "The rise of the networked enterprise: Web 2.0 finds its payday," *McKinsey Quarterly*. December 2010.

23 Michael Chui, Markus Löffler, and Roger Roberts, "The Internet of Things," *McKinsey Quarterly*, March 2010.

connected nodes in the Internet of Things—sometimes also referred to as machine-to-machine (M2M) devices—deployed in the world will grow at a rate exceeding 30 percent annually over the next five years (Exhibit 10). Some of the growth sectors are expected to be utilities as these operators install more smart meters and smart appliances; health care, as the sector deploys remote health monitoring; retail, which will eventually increase its use of radio frequency identification (RFID) tags; and the automotive industry, which will increasingly install sensors in vehicles.

Exhibit 9

The penetration of social networks is increasing online and on smartphones; frequent users are increasing as a share of total users[1]

 Frequent user[2]

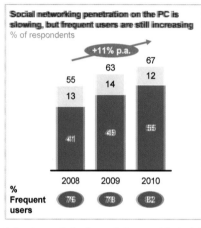

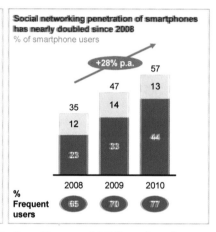

1 Based on penetration of users who browse social network sites. For consistency, we exclude Twitter-specific questions (added to survey in 2009) and location-based mobile social networks (e.g., Foursquare, added to survey in 2010).
2 Frequent users defined as those that use social networking at least once a week.

SOURCE: McKinsey iConsumer Survey

Exhibit 10

Data generated from the Internet of Things will grow exponentially as the number of connected nodes increases

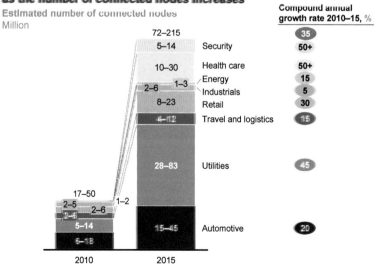

NOTE: Numbers may not sum due to rounding.
SOURCE: Analyst interviews; McKinsey Global Institute analysis

TRADITIONAL USES OF IT HAVE CONTRIBUTED TO PRODUCTIVITY GROWTH— BIG DATA IS THE NEXT FRONTIER

The history of IT investment and innovation and its impact on competitiveness and productivity strongly suggest that big data can have similar power to transform our lives. The same preconditions that enabled IT to power productivity are in place for big data. We believe that there is compelling evidence that the use of big data will become a key basis of competition, underpinning new waves of productivity growth, innovation, and consumer surplus—as long as the right policies and enablers are in place.

Over a number of years, MGI has researched the link between IT and productivity.[24] The same causal relationships apply just as much to big data as they do to IT in general. Big data levers offer significant potential for improving productivity at the level of individual companies. Companies including Tesco, Amazon, Wal-Mart, Harrah's, Progressive Insurance, and Capital One, and Smart, a wireless player in the Philippines, have already wielded the use of big data as a competitive weapon—as have entire economies (see Box 5, "Large companies across the globe have scored early successes in their use of big data").

Box 5. Large companies across the globe have scored early successes in their use of big data

There are notable examples of companies around the globe that are well-known for their extensive and effective use of data. For instance, Tesco's loyalty program generates a tremendous amount of customer data that the company mines to inform decisions from promotions to strategic segmentation of customers. Amazon uses customer data to power its recommendation engine "you may also like …" based on a type of predictive modeling technique called collaborative filtering. By making supply and demand signals visible between retail stores and suppliers, Wal-Mart was an early adopter of vendor-managed inventory to optimize the supply chain. Harrah's, the US hotels and casinos group, compiles detailed holistic profiles of its customers and uses them to tailor marketing in a way that has increased customer loyalty. Progressive Insurance and Capital One are both known for conducting experiments to segment their customers systematically and effectively and to tailor product offers accordingly. Smart, a leading wireless player in the Philippines, analyzes its penetration, retailer coverage, and average revenue per user at the city or town level in order to focus on the micro markets with the most potential.

We can disaggregate the impact of IT on productivity first into productivity growth in IT-producing sectors such as semiconductors, telecoms, and computer manufacturing, and that of IT-using sectors. In general, much of the productivity growth in IT-producing sectors results from improving the quality of IT products as technology develops. In this analysis, we focus largely on the sectors that use IT (and that will increasingly use big data), accounting for a much larger slice of the global economy than the sectors that supply IT.

Research shows that there are two essential preconditions for IT to affect labor productivity. The first is capital deepening—in other words, the IT investments that give

---

24 See *US productivity growth, 1995–2000*, McKinsey Global Institute, October 2001, and *How IT enables productivity growth*, McKinsey Global Institute, October 2002, both available at www.mckinsey.com/mgi.

workers better and faster tools to do their jobs. The second is investment in human capital and organizational change—i.e., managerial innovations that complement IT investments in order to drive labor productivity gains. In some cases, a lag between IT investments and organizational adjustments has meant that productivity improvements have taken awhile to show up. The same preconditions that explain the impact of IT in enabling historical productivity growth currently exist for big data.[25]

There have been four waves of IT adoption with different degrees of impact on productivity growth in the United States (Exhibit 11). The first of these eras—the "mainframe" era—ran from 1959 to 1973. During this period, annual US productivity growth overall was very high at 2.82 percent. IT's contribution to productivity was rather modest; at that stage, IT's share of overall capital expenditure was relatively low. The second era from 1973 to 1995, which we'll call the era of "minicomputers and PCs," experienced much lower growth in overall productivity, but we can attribute a greater share of that growth to the impact of IT. Significant IT capital deepening occurred. Companies began to boost their spending on more distributed types of computers, and these computers became more powerful as their quality increased.

The third era ran from 1995 to 2000—the era of the "Internet and Web 1.0." In this period, US productivity growth returned to high rates, underpinned by significant IT capital deepening, an intensification of improvements in quality, and also the diffusion of significant managerial innovations that took advantage of previous IT capital investment. As we have suggested, there as a lag between IT investment and the managerial innovation necessary to accelerate productivity growth. Indeed, although we have named this era for the investments in Internet and Web 1.0 made at this time, most of the positive impact on productivity in IT-using sectors came from managerial and organizational change in response to investments in previous eras in mainframe, minicomputers, and PCs—and not from investment in the Internet.

MGI research found that in this third era, productivity gains were unevenly distributed at the macroeconomic, sector, and firm levels. In some cases, a leading firm that had invested in sufficient IT was able to deploy managerial innovation to drive productivity and outcompete its industry counterparts. Wal-Mart's implementation of IT-intensive business processes allowed the company to outperform competitors in the retail industry. Eventually those competitors invested in IT in response, accelerated their own productivity growth, and boosted the productivity of the entire sector.

In fact, MGI found that six sectors accounted for almost all of the productivity gains in the US economy, while the rest contributed either very little productivity growth or even, in some cases, negative productivity growth. The six sectors that achieved a leap in productivity shared three broad characteristics in their approach to IT. First, they tailored their IT investment to sector-specific business processes and linked it to key performance levers. Second, they deployed IT sequentially, building capabilities over time. Third, IT investment evolved simultaneously with managerial and technical innovation.

---

25 We draw both on previous MGI research and an analysis by Dale Jorgenson, Mun Ho, and Kevin Stiroh of how IT impacted on US productivity growth between 1959 and 2006. See *US productivity growth, 1995–2000*, October 2001, and *How IT enables productivity growth*, October 2002, both available at www.mckinsey.com/mgi; Dale Jorgenson, Mun Ho, and Kevin Stiroh, "A Retrospective Look at the US Productivity Growth Resurgence," Journal of Economic Perspectives, 2008; and Erik Brynjolfsson and Adam Saunders, *Wired for innovation: How information technology is reshaping the economy* (Cambridge, MA: MIT Press, 2009).

Exhibit 11

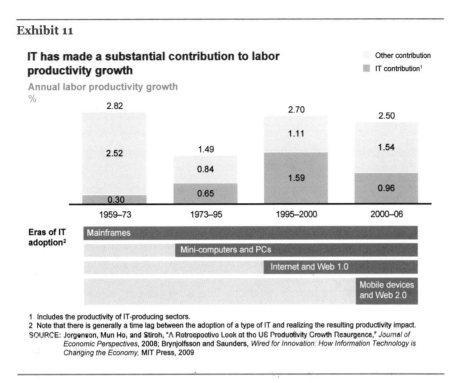

IT has made a substantial contribution to labor productivity growth

Other contribution
IT contribution[1]

Annual labor productivity growth
%

	1959–73	1973–95	1995–2000	2000–06
Total	2.82	1.49	2.70	2.50
Other contribution	2.52	0.84	1.11	1.54
IT contribution	0.30	0.65	1.59	0.96

Eras of IT adoption[2]

Mainframes
Mini-computers and PCs
Internet and Web 1.0
Mobile devices and Web 2.0

1 Includes the productivity of IT-producing sectors.
2 Note that there is generally a time lag between the adoption of a type of IT and realizing the resulting productivity impact.
SOURCE: Jorgenson, Mun Ho, and Stiroh, "A Retrospective Look at the US Productivity Growth Resurgence," *Journal of Economic Perspectives*, 2008; Brynjolfsson and Saunders, *Wired for Innovation: How Information Technology is Changing the Economy*, MIT Press, 2009

The fourth and final era, running from 2000 to 2006, is the period of the "mobile devices and Web 2.0." During this period, the contribution from IT capital deepening and that from IT-producing sectors dropped. However, the contribution from managerial innovations increased—again, this wave of organizational change looks like a lagged response to the investments in Internet and Web 1.0 from the preceding five years.[26]

What do these patterns tell us about prospects for big data and productivity? Like previous waves of IT-enabled productivity, leveraging big data fundamentally requires both IT investments (in storage and processing power) and managerial innovation. It seems likely that data intensity and capital deepening will fuel the diffusion of the complementary managerial innovation boost productivity growth. As of now, there is no empirical evidence of a link between data intensity or capital deepening in data investments and productivity in specific sectors. The story of IT and productivity suggests that the reason for this is a time lag and that we will, at some point, see investments in big-data-related capital deepening pay off in the form of productivity gains.

In the research we conducted into big data in five domains across different geographies, we find strong evidence that big data levers can boost efficiency by reducing the number or size of inputs while retaining the same output level. At the same time, they can be an important means of adding value by producing more real output with no increase in input. In health care, for example, big data levers can boost efficiency by reducing systemwide costs linked to undertreatment and overtreatment and by reducing errors and duplication in treatment. These levers will also improve the quality of care and patient outcomes. Similarly, in public sector administration, big data levers lead to not only efficiency gains, but also gains in effectiveness from enabling governments to collect taxes more efficiently and helping to drive the quality of services from education to unemployment offices. For retailers, big data supply

26 We use multifactor productivity in IT-using industries as our measurement of the impact of managerial innovation.

chain and operations levers can improve the efficiency of the entire sector. Marketing and merchandising levers will help consumers find better products to meet their needs at more reasonable prices, increasing real value added.

The combination of deepening investments in big data and managerial innovation to create competitive advantage and boost productivity is very similar to the way IT developed from the 1970s onward. The experience of IT strongly suggests that we could be on the cusp of a new wave of productivity growth enabled by the use of big data.

□ □ □

Data have become an important factor of production today—on a par with physical assets and human capital—and the increasing intensity with which enterprises are gathering information alongside the rise of multimedia, social media, and the Internet of Things will continue to fuel exponential growth in data for the foreseeable future. Big data have significant potential to create value for both businesses and consumers.

2. Big data techniques and technologies

A wide variety of techniques and technologies has been developed and adapted to aggregate, manipulate, analyze, and visualize big data. These techniques and technologies draw from several fields including statistics, computer science, applied mathematics, and economics. This means that an organization that intends to derive value from big data has to adopt a flexible, multidisciplinary approach. Some techniques and technologies were developed in a world with access to far smaller volumes and variety in data, but have been successfully adapted so that they are applicable to very large sets of more diverse data. Others have been developed more recently, specifically to capture value from big data. Some were developed by academics and others by companies, especially those with online business models predicated on analyzing big data.

This report concentrates on documenting the potential value that leveraging big data can create. It is not a detailed instruction manual on how to capture value, a task that requires highly specific customization to an organization's context, strategy, and capabilities. However, we wanted to note some of the main techniques and technologies that can be applied to harness big data to clarify the way some of the levers for the use of big data that we describe might work. These are not comprehensive lists—the story of big data is still being written; new methods and tools continue to be developed to solve new problems. To help interested readers find a particular technique or technology easily, we have arranged these lists alphabetically. Where we have used bold typefaces, we are illustrating the multiple interconnections between techniques and technologies. We also provide a brief selection of illustrative examples of visualization, a key tool for understanding very large-scale data and complex analyses in order to make better decisions.

TECHNIQUES FOR ANALYZING BIG DATA

There are many techniques that draw on disciplines such as statistics and computer science (particularly machine learning) that can be used to analyze datasets. In this section, we provide a list of some categories of techniques applicable across a range of industries. This list is by no means exhaustive. Indeed, researchers continue to develop new techniques and improve on existing ones, particularly in response to the need to analyze new combinations of data. We note that not all of these techniques strictly require the use of big data—some of them can be applied effectively to smaller datasets (e.g., A/B testing, regression analysis). However, all of the techniques we list here can be applied to big data and, in general, larger and more diverse datasets can be used to generate more numerous and insightful results than smaller, less diverse ones.

A/B testing. A technique in which a control group is compared with a variety of test groups in order to determine what treatments (i.e., changes) will improve a given objective variable, e.g., marketing response rate. This technique is also known as split testing or bucket testing. An example application is determining what copy text, layouts, images, or colors will improve conversion rates on an e-commerce Web site. Big data enables huge numbers of tests to be executed and analyzed, ensuring that groups are of sufficient size to detect meaningful (i.e., statistically significant) differences between the control and treatment groups (see **statistics**). When more than one variable is simultaneously manipulated in the treatment, the multivariate generalization of this technique, which applies statistical modeling, is often called "A/B/N" testing.

Association rule learning. A set of techniques for discovering interesting relationships, i.e., "association rules," among variables in large databases.[27] These techniques consist of a variety of algorithms to generate and test possible rules. One application is market basket analysis, in which a retailer can determine which products are frequently bought together and use this information for marketing (a commonly cited example is the discovery that many supermarket shoppers who buy diapers also tend to buy beer). Used for **data mining**.

Classification. A set of techniques to identify the categories in which new data points belong, based on a training set containing data points that have already been categorized. One application is the prediction of segment-specific customer behavior (e.g., buying decisions, churn rate, consumption rate) where there is a clear hypothesis or objective outcome. These techniques are often described as **supervised learning** because of the existence of a training set; they stand in contrast to **cluster analysis**, a type of unsupervised learning. Used for **data mining**.

Cluster analysis. A statistical method for classifying objects that splits a diverse group into smaller groups of similar objects, whose characteristics of similarity are not known in advance. An example of cluster analysis is segmenting consumers into self-similar groups for targeted marketing. This is a type of **unsupervised learning** because training data are not used. This technique is in contrast to **classification**, a type of supervised learning. Used for **data mining**.

Crowdsourcing. A technique for collecting data submitted by a large group of people or ommunity (i.e., the "crowd") through an open call, usually through networked media such as the Web.[28] This is a type of mass collaboration and an instance of using Web 2.0.[29]

Data fusion and data integration. A set of techniques that integrate and analyze data from multiple sources in order to develop insights in ways that are more efficient and potentially more accurate than if they were developed by analyzing a single source of data. **Signal processing** techniques can be used to implement some types of data fusion. One example of an application is sensor data from the Internet of Things being combined to develop an integrated perspective on the performance of a complex distributed system such as an oil refinery. Data from social media, analyzed by **natural language processing**, can be combined with real-time sales data, in order to determine what effect a marketing campaign is having on customer sentiment and purchasing behavior.

Data mining. A set of techniques to extract patterns from large datasets by combining methods from **statistics** and **machine learning** with database management. These techniques include **association rule learning, cluster analysis, classification**, and **regression**. Applications include mining customer data to determine segments most likely to respond to an offer, mining human

27 R. Agrawal, T. Imielinski, and A. Swami, "Mining association rules between sets of items in large databases," SIGMOD Conference 1993: 207–16; P. Hajek, I. Havel, and M. Chytil, "The GUHA method of automatic hypotheses determination," *Computing* 1(4), 1966; 293–308.

28 Jeff Howe, "The Rise of Crowdsourcing," *Wired*, Issue 14.06, June 2006.

29 Michael Chui, Andy Miller, and Roger Roberts, "Six ways to make Web 2.0 work," *McKinsey Quarterly*, February 2009.

resources data to identify characteristics of most successful employees, or market basket analysis to model the purchase behavior of customers.

Ensemble learning. Using multiple **predictive models** (each developed using **statistics** and/or **machine learning**) to obtain better predictive performance than could be obtained from any of the constituent models. This is a type of **supervised learning**.

Genetic algorithms. A technique used for **optimization** that is inspired by the process of natural evolution or "survival of the fittest." In this technique, potential solutions are encoded as "chromosomes" that can combine and mutate. These individual chromosomes are selected for survival within a modeled "environment" that determines the fitness or performance of each individual in the population. Often described as a type of "evolutionary algorithm," these algorithms are well-suited for solving nonlinear problems. Examples of applications include improving job scheduling in manufacturing and optimizing the performance of an investment portfolio.

Machine learning. A subspecialty of computer science (within a field historically called "artificial intelligence") concerned with the design and development of algorithms that allow computers to evolve behaviors based on empirical data. A major focus of machine learning research is to automatically learn to recognize complex patterns and make intelligent decisions based on data. **Natural language processing** is an example of machine learning.

Natural language processing (NLP). A set of techniques from a subspecialty of computer science (within a field historically called "artificial intelligence") and linguistics that uses computer algorithms to analyze human (natural) language. Many NLP techniques are types of machine learning. One application of NLP is using **sentiment analysis** on social media to determine how prospective customers are reacting to a branding campaign.

Neural networks. Computational models, inspired by the structure and workings of biological neural networks (i.e., the cells and connections within a brain), that find patterns in data. Neural networks are well-suited for finding nonlinear patterns. They can be used for **pattern recognition** and **optimization**. Some neural network applications involve supervised learning and others involve unsupervised learning. Examples of applications include identifying high-value customers that are at risk of leaving a particular company and identifying fraudulent insurance claims.

Network analysis. A set of techniques used to characterize relationships among discrete nodes in a graph or a network. In social network analysis, connections between individuals in a community or organization are analyzed, e.g., how information travels, or who has the most influence over whom. Examples of applications include identifying key opinion leaders to target for marketing, and identifying bottlenecks in enterprise information flows.

Optimization. A portfolio of numerical techniques used to redesign complex systems and processes to improve their performance according to one or more objective measures (e.g., cost, speed, or reliability). Examples of applications include improving operational processes such as scheduling, routing, and floor layout, and making strategic decisions such as product range strategy, linked investment analysis, and R&D portfolio strategy. **Genetic algorithms** are an example of an optimization technique.

Pattern recognition. A set of machine learning techniques that assign some sort of output value (or *label*) to a given input value (or *instance*) according to a specific algorithm. **Classification** techniques are an example.

Predictive modeling. A set of techniques in which a mathematical model is created or chosen to best predict the probability of an outcome. An example of an application in customer relationship management is the use of predictive models to estimate the likelihood that a customer will "churn" (i.e., change providers) or the likelihood that a customer can be cross-sold another product. **Regression** is one example of the many predictive modeling techniques.

Regression. A set of statistical techniques to determine how the value of the dependent variable changes when one or more independent variables is modified. Often used for forecasting or prediction. Examples of applications include forecasting sales volumes based on various market and economic variables or determining what measurable manufacturing parameters most influence customer satisfaction. Used for **data mining**.

Sentiment analysis. Application of **natural language processing** and other analytic techniques to identify and extract subjective information from source text material. Key aspects of these analyses include identifying the feature, aspect, or product about which a sentiment is being expressed, and determining the type, "polarity" (i.e., positive, negative, or neutral) and the degree and strength of the sentiment. Examples of applications include companies applying sentiment analysis to analyze social media (e.g., blogs, microblogs, and social networks) to determine how different customer segments and stakeholders are reacting to their products and actions.

Signal processing. A set of techniques from electrical engineering and applied mathematics originally developed to analyze discrete and continuous signals, i.e., representations of analog physical quantities (even if represented digitally) such as radio signals, sounds, and images. This category includes techniques from signal detection theory, which quantifies the ability to discern between signal and noise. Sample applications include modeling for **time series analysis** or implementing **data fusion** to determine a more precise reading by combining data from a set of less precise data sources (i.e., extracting the signal from the noise).

Spatial analysis. A set of techniques, some applied from **statistics**, which analyze the topological, geometric, or geographic properties encoded in a data set. Often the data for spatial analysis come from geographic information systems (GIS) that capture data including location information, e.g., addresses or latitude/longitude coordinates. Examples of applications include the incorporation of spatial data into spatial **regressions** (e.g., how is consumer willingness to purchase a product correlated with location?) or **simulations** (e.g., how would a manufacturing supply chain network perform with sites in different locations?).

Statistics. The science of the collection, organization, and interpretation of data, including the design of surveys and experiments. Statistical techniques are often used to make judgments about what relationships between variables could have occurred by chance (the "null hypothesis"), and what relationships between variables likely result from some kind of underlying causal relationship (i.e., that are "statistically significant"). Statistical techniques are also used to reduce the likelihood of Type I errors ("false positives") and Type II errors ("false negatives"). An example of an application is **A/B testing** to determine what types of marketing material will most increase revenue.

Supervised learning. The set of machine learning techniques that infer a function or relationship from a set of training data. Examples include **classification** and support vector machines.[30] This is different from **unsupervised learning**.

Simulation. Modeling the behavior of complex systems, often used for forecasting, predicting and scenario planning. Monte Carlo simulations, for example, are a class of algorithms that rely on repeated random sampling, i.e., running thousands of simulations, each based on different assumptions. The result is a histogram that gives a probability distribution of outcomes. One application is assessing the likelihood of meeting financial targets given uncertainties about the success of various initiatives.

Time series analysis. Set of techniques from both **statistics** and **signal processing** for analyzing sequences of data points, representing values at successive times, to extract meaningful characteristics from the data. Examples of time series analysis include the hourly value of a stock market index or the number of patients diagnosed with a given condition every day. Time series forecasting is the use of a model to predict future values of a time series based on known past values of the same or other series. Some of these techniques, e.g., structural modeling, decompose a series into trend, seasonal, and residual components, which can be useful for identifying cyclical patterns in the data. Examples of applications include forecasting sales figures, or predicting the number of people who will be diagnosed with an infectious disease.

Unsupervised learning. A set of machine learning techniques that finds hidden structure in unlabeled data. **Cluster analysis** is an example of unsupervised learning (in contrast to **supervised learning**).

Visualization. Techniques used for creating images, diagrams, or animations to communicate, understand, and improve the results of big data analyses (see the last section of this chapter).

BIG DATA TECHNOLOGIES

There is a growing number of technologies used to aggregate, manipulate, manage, and analyze big data. We have detailed some of the more prominent technologies but this list is not exhaustive, especially as more technologies continue to be developed to support big data techniques, some of which we have listed.

Big Table. Proprietary distributed database system built on the **Google File System**. Inspiration for **HBase**.

Business intelligence (BI). A type of application software designed to report, analyze, and present data. BI tools are often used to read data that have been previously stored in a **data warehouse** or **data mart**. BI tools can also be used to create standard reports that are generated on a periodic basis, or to display information on real-time management dashboards, i.e., integrated displays of metrics that measure the performance of a system.

Cassandra. An open source (free) database management system designed to handle huge amounts of data on a **distributed system**. This system was originally developed at Facebook and is now managed as a project of the Apache Software foundation.

30 Corinna Cortes and Vladimir Vapnik, "Support-vector networks," *Machine Learning* 20(3), September 1995 (www.springerlink.com/content/k238jx04hm87j80g/).

Cloud computing. A computing paradigm in which highly scalable computing resources, often configured as a distributed system, are provided as a service through a network.

Data mart. Subset of a data warehouse, used to provide data to users usually through **business intelligence** tools.

Data warehouse. Specialized database optimized for reporting, often used for storing large amounts of structured data. Data is uploaded using **ETL (extract, transform, and load)** tools from operational data stores, and reports are often generated using **business intelligence** tools.

Distributed system. Multiple computers, communicating through a network, used to solve a common computational problem. The problem is divided into multiple tasks, each of which is solved by one or more computers working in parallel. Benefits of distributed systems include higher performance at a lower cost (i.e., because a cluster of lower-end computers can be less expensive than a single higher-end computer), higher reliability (i.e., because of a lack of a single point of failure), and more scalability (i.e., because increasing the power of a distributed system can be accomplished by simply adding more nodes rather than completely replacing a central computer).

Dynamo. Proprietary distributed data storage system developed by Amazon.

Extract, transform, and load (ETL). Software tools used to extract data from outside sources, transform them to fit operational needs, and load them into a database or data warehouse.

Google File System. Proprietary distributed file system developed by Google; part of the inspiration for **Hadoop**.[31]

Hadoop. An open source (free) software framework for processing huge datasets on certain kinds of problems on a distributed system. Its development was inspired by Google's **MapReduce** and **Google File System**. It was originally developed at Yahoo! and is now managed as a project of the Apache Software Foundation.

HBase. An open source (free), distributed, non-relational database modeled on Google's **Big Table**. It was originally developed by Powerset and is now managed as a project of the Apache Software foundation as part of the **Hadoop**.

MapReduce. A software framework introduced by Google for processing huge datasets on certain kinds of problems on a distributed system.[32] Also implemented in **Hadoop**.

Mashup. An application that uses and combines data presentation or functionality from two or more sources to create new services. These applications are often made available on the Web, and frequently use data accessed through open application programming interfaces or from open data sources.

Metadata. Data that describes the content and context of data files, e.g., means of creation, purpose, time and date of creation, and author.

31 Sanjay Ghemawat, Howard Gobioff, and Shun-Tak Leung, "The Google file system," 19th ACM Symposium on Operating Systems Principles, Lake George, NY, October 2003 (labs.google. com/papers/gfs.html).

32 Jeffrey Dean and Sanjay Ghemawat, "MapReduce: Simplified data processing on large clusters," Sixth Symposium on Operating System Design and Implementation, San Francisco, CA, December 2004 (labs.google.com/papers/mapreduce.html).

Non-relational database. A database that does not store data in tables (rows and columns). (In contrast to **relational database**).

R. An open source (free) programming language and software environment for statistical computing and graphics. The R language has become a de facto standard among statisticians for developing statistical software and is widely used for statistical software development and data analysis. R is part of the GNU Project, a collaboration that supports open source projects.

Relational database. A database made up of a collection of tables (relations), i.e., data are stored in rows and columns. Relational database management systems (RDBMS) store a type of structured data. **SQL** is the most widely used language for managing relational databases (see item below).

Semi-structured data. Data that do not conform to fixed fields but contain tags and other markers to separate data elements. Examples of semi-structured data include XML or HTML-tagged text. Contrast with **structured data** and **unstructured data**.

SQL. Originally an acronym for structured query language, SQL is a computer language designed for managing data in **relational databases**. This technique includes the ability to insert, query, update, and delete data, as well as manage data schema (database structures) and control access to data in the database.

Stream processing. Technologies designed to process large real-time streams of event data. Stream processing enables applications such as algorithmic trading in financial services, RFID event processing applications, fraud detection, process monitoring, and location-based services in telecommunications. Also known as event stream processing.

Structured data. Data that reside in fixed fields. Examples of structured data include **relational databases** or data in spreadsheets. Contrast with **semi-structured data** and **unstructured data**.

Unstructured data. Data that do not reside in fixed fields. Examples include free-form text (e.g., books, articles, body of e-mail messages), untagged audio, image and video data. Contrast with structured data and semi-structured data.

Visualization. Technologies used for creating images, diagrams, or animations to communicate a message that are often used to synthesize the results of big data analyses (see the next section for examples).

VISUALIZATION

Presenting information in such a way that people can consume it effectively is a key challenge that needs to be met if analyzing data is to lead to concrete action. As we discussed in box 4, human beings have evolved to become highly effective at perceiving certain types of patterns with their senses but continue to face significant constraints in their ability to process other types of data such as large amounts of numerical or text data. For this reason, there is a currently a tremendous amount of research and innovation in the field of visualization, i.e., techniques and technologies used for creating images, diagrams, or animations to communicate, understand, and improve the results of big data analyses. We present some examples to provide a glimpse into this burgeoning and important field that supports big data.

34

Tag cloud

This graphic is a visualization of the text of this report in the form of a tag cloud, i.e., a weighted visual list, in which words that appear most frequently are larger and words that appear less frequently smaller. This type of visualization helps the reader to quickly perceive the most salient concepts in a large body of text.

agencies analysis analytical applications business care clinical companies consumers costs create customer data developed digital economy example exhibit global government growth health improve including increasing industry information levers location management manufacturing organizations percent performance personal policy potential productivity providers public research retail sector services talent techniques technology united used value

Clustergram

A clustergram is a visualization technique used for cluster analysis displaying how individual members of a dataset are assigned to clusters as the number of clusters increases.[33] The choice of the number of clusters is an important parameter in cluster analysis. This technique enables the analyst to reach a better understanding of how the results of clustering vary with different numbers of clusters.

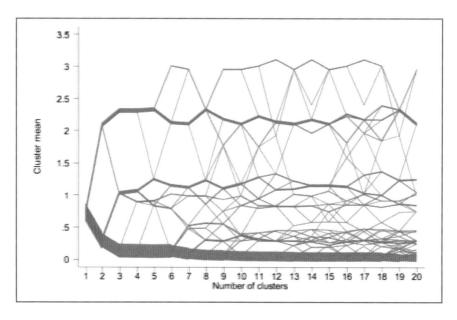

33 Matthias Schonlau, "The clustergram: a graph for visualizing hierarchical and non-hierarchical cluster analyses," *The Stata Journal*, 2002; 2 (4): 391-402.

History flow

History flow is a visualization technique that charts the evolution of a document as it is edited by multiple contributing authors.[34] Time appears on the horizontal axis, while contributions to to the text are on the vertical axis; each author has a different color code and the vertical length of a bar indicates the amount of text written by each author. By visualizing the history of a document in this manner, various insights easily emerge. For instance, the history flow we show here that depicts the Wikipedia entry for the word "Islam" shows that an increasing number of authors have made contributions over the history of this entry.[35] One can also see easily that the length of the document has grown over time as more authors have elaborated on the topic, but that, at certain points, there have been significant deletions, too, i.e., when the vertical length has decreased. One can even see instances of "vandalism" in which the document has been removed completely although, interestingly, the document has tended to be repaired and returned to its previous state very quickly.

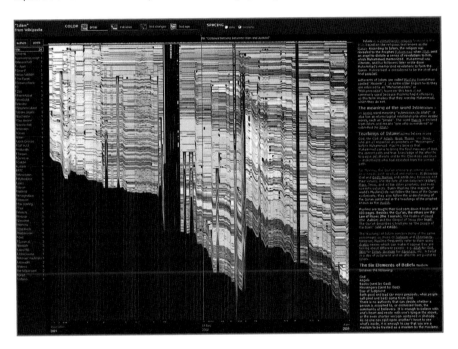

---

34 Fernanda B. Viegas, Martin Wattenberg, and Kushal Dave, *Studying cooperation and conflict between authors with history flow visualizations*, CHI2004 proceedings of the SIGCHI conference on human factors in computing systems, 2004.

35 For more examples of history flows, see the gallery provided by the Collaborative User Experience Research group of IBM (www.research.ibm.com/visual/projects/history_flow/gallery.htm).

Spatial information flow

Another visualization technique is one that depicts spatial information flows. The example we show here is entitled the New York Talk Exchange.[36] It shows the amount of Internet Protocol (IP) data flowing between New York and cities around the world. The size of the glow on a particular city location corresponds to the amount of IP traffic flowing between that place and New York City; the greater the glow, the larger the flow. This visualization allows us to determine quickly which cities are most closely connected to New York in terms of their communications volume.

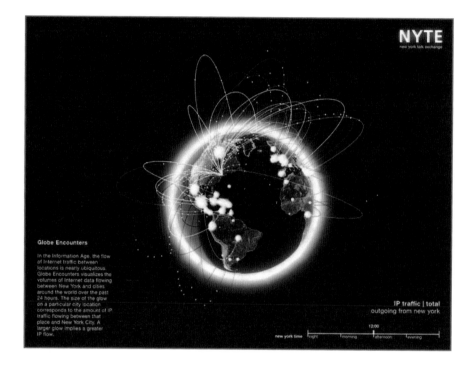

36 The New York Talk Exchange was displayed at New York's Museum of Modern Art in 2008 (senseable.mit.edu/nyte/).

3. The transformative potential of big data in five domains

To explore how big data can create value and the size of this potential, we chose five domains to study in depth: health care in the United States; public sector administration in the European Union; retail in the United States; global manufacturing; and global personal location data.

Together these five represented close to 40 percent of global GDP in 2010 (Exhibit 12).[37] In the course of our analysis of these domains, we conducted interviews with industry experts and undertook a thorough review of current literature. For each domain, we identified specific levers through which big data can create value; quantified the potential for additional value; and cataloged the enablers necessary for companies, organizations, governments, and individuals to capture that value.

The five domains vary in their sophistication and maturity in the use of big data and therefore offer different business lessons. They also represent a broad spectrum of key segments of the global economy and capture a range of regional perspectives. They include globally tradable sectors such as manufacturing and nontradable sectors such as public sector administration, as well as a mix of products and services.

Health care is a large and important segment of the US economy that faces tremendous productivity challenges. It has multiple and varied stakeholders, including the pharmaceutical and medical products industries, providers, payors, and patients. Each of these has different interests and business incentives while still being closely intertwined. Each generates pools of data, but they have typically remained unconnected from each other. A significant portion of clinical data is not yet digitized. There is a substantial opportunity to create value if these pools of data can be digitized, combined, and used effectively. However, the incentives to leverage big data in this sector are often out of alignment, offering an instructive case on the sector-wide interventions that can be necessary to capture value.

The public sector is another large part of the global economy facing tremendous pressure to improve its productivity. Governments have access to large pools of digital data but, in general, have hardly begun to take advantage of the powerful ways in which they could use this information to improve performance and transparency. We chose to study the administrative parts of government. This is a domain where there is a great deal of data, which gives us the opportunity to draw analogies with processes in other knowledge worker industries such as claims processing in insurance.

In contrast to the first two domains, retail is a sector in which some players have been using big data for some time for segmenting customers and managing supply chains. Nevertheless, there is still tremendous upside potential across the industry for individual players to expand and improve their use of big data, particularly given the increasing ease with which they can collect information on their consumers, suppliers, and inventories.

---

37 For more details on the methodology that we used in our case studies, see the appendix.

Manufacturing offers a detailed look at a globally traded industry with often complex and widely distributed value chains and a large amount of data available. This domain therefore offers an examination at multiple points in the value chain, from bringing products to market and research and development (R&D) to after-sales services.

Personal location data is a nascent domain that cuts across industry sectors from telecom to media to transportation. The data generated are growing quickly, reflecting the burgeoning adoption of smartphones and other applications. This domain is a hotbed of innovation that could transform organizations and the lives of individuals, potentially creating a significant amount of surplus for consumers.

Exhibit 12

The five sectors or domains we have chosen to study in depth make important contributions to the global economy

Estimated global GDP of sectors in 2010
% of total GDP

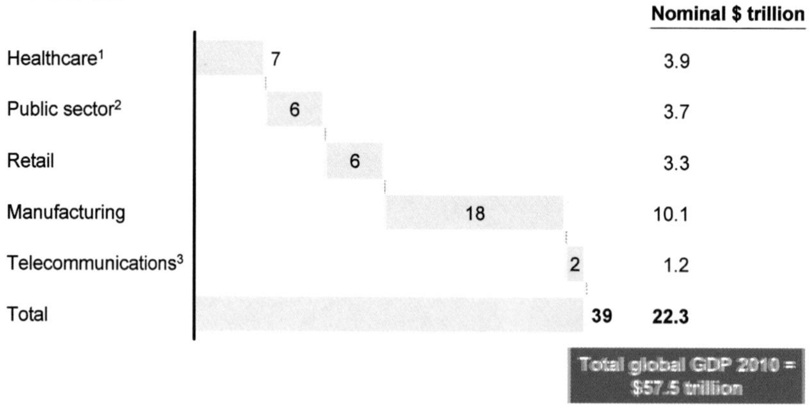

		Nominal $ trillion
Healthcare[1]	7	3.9
Public sector[2]	6	3.7
Retail	6	3.3
Manufacturing	18	10.1
Telecommunications[3]	2	1.2
Total	39	22.3

Total global GDP 2010 = $57.5 trillion

1 Includes health and social services, medical and measuring equipment, and pharmaceuticals.
2 Refers to public sector administration, defense, and compulsory social security (excludes education).
3 Since personal location data is a domain and not a sector, we've used telecom as a comparison for GDP.
NOTE: Numbers may not sum due to rounding.
SOURCE: Global Insight; McKinsey Global Institute analysis

3a. Health care (United States)

Reforming the US health care system to reduce the rate at which costs have been increasing while sustaining its current strengths is critical to the United States both as a society and as an economy. Health care, one of the largest sectors of the US economy, accounts for slightly more than 17 percent of GDP and employs an estimated 11 percent of the country's workers. It is becoming clear that the historic rate of growth of US health care expenditures, increasing annually by nearly 5 percent in real terms over the last decade, is unsustainable and is a major contributor to the high national debt levels projected to develop over the next two decades. An aging US population and the emergence of new, more expensive treatments will amplify this trend. Thus far, health care has lagged behind other industries in improving operational performance and adopting technology-enabled process improvements. The magnitude of the problem and potentially long timelines for implementing change make it imperative that decisive measures aimed at increasing productivity begin in the near term to ease escalating cost pressures.

It is possible to address these challenges by emulating and implementing best practices in health care, pioneered in the United States and in other countries. Doing so will often require the analysis of large datasets. MGI studied the health care sector in the United States, where we took an expansive view to include the provider, payor, and pharmaceutical and medical products (PMP) subsectors to understand how big data can help to improve the effectiveness and efficiency of health care as an entire system. Some of the actions that can help stem the rising costs of US health care while improving its quality don't necessarily require big data. These include, for example, tackling major underlying issues such as the high incidence and costs of lifestyle and behavior-induced disease, minimizing any economic distortion between consumers and providers, and reducing the administrative complexity in payors.[38] However, the use of large datasets underlies another set of levers that have the potential to play a major role in more effective and cost-saving care initiatives, the emergence of better products and services, and the creation of new business models in health care and its associated industries. But deploying big data in these areas would need to be accompanied by a range of enablers, some of which would require a substantial rethinking of the way health care is provided and funded.

Our estimates of the potential value that big data can create in health care are therefore not predictions of what will happen but our view on the full economic potential, assuming that required IT and dataset investments, analytical capabilities, privacy protections, and appropriate economic incentives are put in place. With this caveat, we estimate that in about ten years, there is an opportunity to capture more than $300 billion annually in new value, with two-thirds of that in the form of reductions to national health care expenditure—about 8 percent of estimated health care spending at 2010 levels.

US HEALTH CARE COSTS ARE OUTPACING ECONOMIC GROWTH

The United States spends more per person on health care than any other nation in the world—without obvious evidence of better outcomes. Over the next decade, average annual health spending growth is expected to outpace average annual growth in

38 Paul D. Mango and Vivian E. Riefberg, "Three imperatives for improving US health care," *McKinsey Quarterly* December 2008.

GDP by almost 2 percentage points.[39] Available evidence suggests that a substantial share of US spending on health care contributes little to better health outcomes. Multiple studies have found that the United States spends about 30 percent more on care than the average Organisation for Economic Co-operation and Development (OECD) country when adjusted for per capita GDP and relative wealth.[40] Yet the United States still falls below OECD averages on such health care parameters as average life expectancy and infant mortality. The additional spending above OECD trends totals an estimated $750 billion a year out of a national health budget in 2007 of $2.24 trillion—that's about $2,500 per person per year (Exhibit 13). Age, disease burden, and health outcomes cannot account for the significant difference.

Exhibit 13

A comparison with OECD countries suggests that the total economic potential for efficiency improvements is about $750 billion

Per capita health expenditure and per capita GDP, OECD countries, 2007
$ purchasing power parity (PPP)

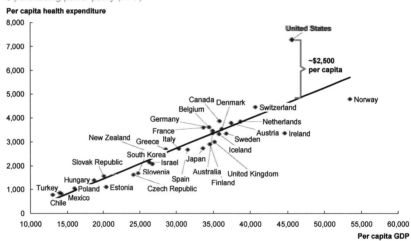

SOURCE: Organisation for Economic Co-operation and Development (OECD)

The current reimbursement system does not create incentives for doctors, hospitals, and other providers of health care—or even their patients—to optimize efficiency or control costs. As currently constructed, the system generally pays for procedures without regard to their effectiveness and necessity. Significantly slowing the growth of health care spending will require fundamental changes in today's incentives. Examples of integrated care models in the United States and beyond demonstrate that, when incentives are aligned and the necessary enablers are in place, the impact of leveraging big data can be very significant (see Box 6, "Health care systems in the United States and beyond have shown early success in their use of big data").

39 Centers for Medicare and Medicaid Services, *National Health Expenditure Projections 2009–2019*, September 2010.

40 These studies adjust for relative health using purchasing power parity. For more detail, see *Accounting for the cost of US health care: A new look at why Americans spend more*, McKinsey Global Institute, December 2008 (www.mckinsey.com/mgi); Chris L. Peterson and Rachel Burton, *US health care spending: Comparison with other OECD countries*, Congressional Research Service, September 2007; Mark Pearson, OECD Health Division, *Written statement to Senate Special Committee on Aging*, September 2009.

Box 6. Health care systems in the United States and beyond have shown early success in their use of big data

The fiscal pressures imposed by rising health care costs have motivated the creation of a promising range of pilot programs in the United States and beyond that use big data and its analytical and management levers to capture real medium- and long-term value. Examples of such innovations include:

- The Department of Veterans Affairs (VA) in the United States has successfully demonstrated several health care information technology (HIT) and remote patient monitoring programs. The VA health system generally outperforms the private sector in following recommended processes for patient care, adhering to clinical guidelines, and achieving greater rates of evidence-based drug therapy. These achievements are largely possible because of the VA's performance-based accountability framework and disease-management practices enabled by electronic medical records (EMR) and HIT.

- The California-based integrated managed-care consortium Kaiser Permanente connected clinical and cost data early on, thus providing the crucial dataset that led to the discovery of Vioxx's adverse drug effects and the subsequent withdrawal of the drug from the market.[1]

- The National Institute for Health and Clinical Excellence, part of the United Kingdom's National Health Service, has pioneered the use of large clinical datasets to investigate the clinical and cost effectiveness of new drugs and expensive existing treatments. The agency issues appropriate guidelines on such costs for the National Health Service and often negotiates prices and market-access conditions with PMP industries.

- The Italian Medicines Agency collects and analyzes clinical data on the experience of expensive new drugs as part of a national cost-effectiveness program. The agency can impose "conditional reimbursement" status on new drugs and can then reevaluate prices and market-access conditions in light of the results of its clinical data studies.

---

1   Merck was granted FDA approval to market Vioxx (rofecoxib) in May 1999. In the five years that elapsed before Merck withdrew Vioxx from the market, an estimated 80 million patients took the drug, making it a "blockbuster" with more than $2 billion per year in sales. Despite statistical evidence in a number of small-scale studies (analyzed later in a metastudy), it took more than five years until the cardiovascular risks of Vioxx were proven. In August 2004, a paper at an International Pharmacoepidemiology meeting in Bordeaux, France, reported the results of a study involving a large Kaiser Permanente database that compared the risk of adverse cardiovascular events for users of Vioxx against the risk for users of Pfizer's Celebrex. The study concluded that more than 27,000 myocardial infarction (heart attack) and sudden cardiac deaths occurred between 1999 and 2003 that could have been avoided. Taking 25 milligrams per day or more of Vioxx resulted in more than three times the risk of acute heart attacks or sudden cardiac death compared with Celebrex use. On September 30, 2004, in what many observers called the largest drug recall in the history of medicine, Merck pulled Vioxx from pharmacy shelves.

US HEALTH CARE HAS FOUR MAIN POOLS OF DATA

The US health care system has four major pools of data within health care, each primarily held by a different constituency. Data are highly fragmented in this domain. The four pools are provider clinical data, payor activity (claims) and cost data, pharmaceutical and medical products R&D data, and patient behavior and sentiment data (Exhibit 14). The amount of data that is available, collected, and analyzed varies widely within the sector. For instance, health providers usually have extensively digitized financial and administrative data, including accounting and basic patient information. In general, however, providers are still at an early stage in digitizing and aggregating clinical data covering such areas as the progress and outcomes of treatments. Depending on the care setting, we estimate that as much as 30 percent of clinical text/numerical data in the United States, including medical records, bills, and laboratory and surgery reports, is still not generated electronically. Even when clinical data are in digital form, they are usually held by an individual provider and rarely shared. Indeed, the majority of clinical data actually generated are in the form of video and monitor feeds, which are used in real time and not stored.

Exhibit 14

Four distinct big data pools exist in the US health care domain today with little overlap in ownership and low integration

Data pools

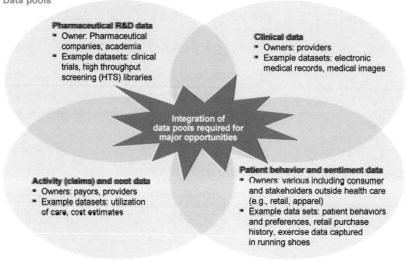

SOURCE: McKinsey Global Institute analysis

There is a strong political push in the United States to deploy electronic health records (EHR)—sometimes referred to as electronic medical records (EMR)—more widely in provider settings. The American Recovery and Reinvestment Act of 2009 included $20 billion in stimulus funding over five years to encourage the meaningful use of EHR by physicians and hospitals. Outcomes-based reimbursement plans could also encourage the deployment of EHR because they would require accurate and complete databases and analytical tools to measure outcomes.

Payors, meanwhile, have been capturing activity (claims) and cost data digitally for many years. Nevertheless, the information is not generally in a form that payors can use for the kind of advanced analysis necessary to generate real insights because it is rarely standardized, often fragmented, or generated in legacy IT systems with incompatible formats.

The PMP subsector is arguably the most advanced in the digitization and use of data in the health care sector. PMP captures R&D data digitally and already analyzes them extensively. Additional opportunities could come from combining PMP data with other datasets such as genomics or proteomics data for personal medicine, or clinical datasets from providers to identify expanded applications and adverse effects.

In addition to clinical, activity (claims) cost data, and pharmaceutical R&D datasets, there is an emerging pool of data related to patient behavior (e.g., propensity to change lifestyle behavior) and sentiment (e.g., from social media) that is potentially valuable but is not held by the health care sector. Patient behavior and sentiment data could be used to influence adherence to treatment regimes, affect lifestyle factors, and influence a broad range of wellness activities.

Many of the levers we identify in the next section involve the integration of multiple data pools. It will be imperative for organizations, and possibly policy makers, to figure out how to align economic incentives and overcome technology barriers to enable the sharing of data.

US HEALTH CARE CAN TAP MULTIPLE BIG DATA LEVERS

We have identified a set of 15 levers in five broad categories that have the potential to improve the efficiency and effectiveness of the health care sector by exploiting the tremendous amount of electronic information that is, and could become, available throughout the US health care sector. Where possible, we estimate the financial potential of deploying these levers in the form of cost savings, increased efficiencies, improved treatment effectiveness, and productivity enhancement. We have arrived at these estimates by referring to international and US best practices (see the appendix for more details). Assuming that the US health care system removes structural barriers and puts the right incentives in place for different stakeholders, we estimate that big data can help to unlock more than $300 billion a year in additional value throughout the sector. The amount that the sector will capture in reality will depend on the collective actions of health care organizations and policy makers in overcoming structural and other barriers.

We focus on levers that require the analysis of large datasets that relate primarily to the development and provision of care, rather than all HIT levers such as automation in claims processing. Our estimates do not aim to capture the entirety of the value generated by HIT (e.g., we exclude value that does not fundamentally require the analysis of large datasets, such as the time saved by doctors and nurses in transcribing notes through the use of EMR or the efficiency savings and increased access to care through mobile health). To validate our findings, we have compared our estimates with those made by other researchers and found them to be comparable (see the appendix).

We divide the levers into five broad categories: clinical operations, payment/pricing, R&D, new business models, and public health. We now discuss each in turn:

Clinical operations

Within clinical operations are five big data levers that mainly affect the way providers, payors, and PMP provide clinical care. We estimate that, if fully employed, these five levers could reduce national health care expenditure by up to $165 billion a year from a base of $2.5 trillion in 2009.

1. **Comparative effectiveness research.** Outcomes-based research determines which treatments will work best for specific patients ("optimal treatment pathways") by analyzing comprehensive patient and outcome data to compare the effectiveness of various interventions. This research includes what is known as comparative effectiveness research (CER). Many studies have shown that wide variations exist in health care practices, outcomes, and costs across different providers, geographies, and patients. Critically analyzing large datasets that include patient characteristics and the cost and outcomes of treatments can help to identify the most clinically effective and cost-effective treatments to apply. If the health care system implements CER, there is potential to reduce incidences of overtreatment—i.e., interventions that do more harm than good—and undertreatment—cases in which a specific therapy should have been prescribed but was not. Both overtreatment and undertreatment result in worse patient outcomes and higher health care costs in the long run.

   Around the world, agencies such as NICE in the United Kingdom, the Institut für Qualität und Wirtschaftlichkeit im Gesundheitswesen (Institute for Quality and Efficiency in Health Care, or IQWIG) in Germany, the Common Drug Review in Canada, and Australia's Pharmaceutical Benefits Scheme have begun CER programs with successful results. The United States took a first step in this direction through the American Recovery and Reinvestment Act of 2009. The law created the Federal Coordinating Council for Comparative Effectiveness Research, which, as its name implies, coordinates comparative effectiveness research across the federal government and makes recommendations for the $400 million allocated for CER. If this lever is to achieve systemwide scale in the United States, it needs to overcome some significant barriers. Comprehensive and consistent clinical and claims datasets need to be captured, integrated, and made available to researchers, and a number of potential issues need to be negotiated. For example, in the current rush to deploy EHR, a potential lack of standards and interoperability could make it difficult to combine datasets. Another concern is how to ensure patient privacy while still providing sufficiently detailed data to allow effective analyses. Having identified optimal treatment pathways, payors will need to be allowed to tie reimbursement decisions and the design of benefits to the results of this research. However, current US law prohibits the Centers for Medicare and Medicaid Services from using the cost/benefit ratio for reimbursement decisions. Disseminating knowledge about the most effective treatments to medical professionals will require the introduction or upgrade of tools, including clinical decision support systems (see the next lever), so that physicians can receive recommendations of best practices at the point of actual decision making about treatments.

2. **Clinical decision support systems.** The second lever is deploying clinical decision support systems for enhancing the efficiency and quality of operations. These systems include computerized physician order-entry capabilities. The current generation of such systems analyzes physician entries and compares them against medical guidelines to alert for potential errors such as adverse drug reactions or events. By deploying these systems, providers can reduce adverse reactions and lower treatment error rates and liability claims, especially those arising from clinical mistakes. In one particularly powerful study conducted at a pediatric critical care unit in a major US metropolitan area, a clinical decision support system tool cut adverse drug reactions and events by 40 percent in just two months.[41]

41 Amy L. Potts, Frederick E. Barr, David F. Gregory, Lorianne Wright, and Neal R. Patel, "Computerized physician order entry and medication errors in a pediatric critical care unit," *Pediatrics* 113(1), 2004: 59–63.

In the future, big data systems such as these can become substantially more intelligent by including modules that use image analysis and recognition in databases of medical images (X-ray, CT, MRI) for prediagnosis or that automatically mine medical literature to create a medical expertise database capable of suggesting treatment options to physicians based on patients' medical records. In addition, clinical decision support systems can enable a larger portion of work to flow to nurse practitioners and physician assistants by automating and facilitating the physician advisory role and thereby improving the efficiency of patient care.

3. **Transparency about medical data.** The third clinical big data lever is analyzing data on medical procedures and creating transparency around those data both to identify performance opportunities for medical professionals, processes, and institutions and to help patients shop for the care that offers the best value.

   Operational and performance datasets from provider settings can be analyzed to create process maps and dashboards enabling information transparency. The goal is to identify and analyze sources of variability and waste in clinical processes and then optimize processes. Mapping processes and physical flows as well as "patient journeys" within an organization can help to reduce delays in the system. Simply publishing cost, quality, and performance data, even without a tangible financial reward, often creates the competition that drives improvements in performance. The operational streamlining resulting from these analyses can produce reduced costs through lean processes, additional revenue potential from freed-up capacity, more efficient staffing that matches demand, improved quality of care, and better patient experiences. The Centers for Medicare and Medicaid Services is testing dashboards as part of an initiative to implement open government principles of transparency, public participation, and collaboration. In the same spirit, the Centers for Disease Control and Prevention has begun publishing health data in an interactive format and providing advanced features for manipulating its pretabulated data.

   Publishing quality and performance data can also help patients make more informed health care decisions compared with the situation today in which differences in cost and quality are largely opaque to them.[42] Transparency about the data on cost and quality, along with appropriate reimbursement schemes (e.g., where patients' out-of-pocket expenses are tied to the actual costs charged by the providers) will encourage patients to take a more value-conscious approach to consuming health care, which in turn will help make providers more competitive and ultimately improve the overall performance of the sector.

4. **Remote patient monitoring.** The fourth clinical big data lever is collecting data from remote patient monitoring for chronically ill patients and analyzing the resulting data to monitor adherence (determining if patients are actually doing what was prescribed) and to improve future drug and treatment options. An estimated 150 million patients in the United States in 2010 were chronically ill with diseases such as diabetes, congestive heart failure, and hypertension, and they accounted for more than 80 percent of health system costs that year. Remote patient monitoring systems can be highly useful for treating such patients. The systems include devices that monitor heart conditions, send information about blood-sugar levels, transmit feedback from caregivers, and even include "chip-on-a-pill" technology—pharmaceuticals that act as instruments to report when they are ingested by a patient—that feeds data in near real time to electronic

---

42 Cost differences can be quite substantial. For example, the cost of a colonoscopy can vary by a factor of six *within* the San Francisco area.

medical record databases. Simply alerting a physician that a congestive heart failure patient is gaining weight because of water retention can prevent an emergency hospitalization. More generally, the use of data from remote monitoring systems can reduce patient in-hospital bed days, cut emergency department visits, improve the targeting of nursing home care and outpatient physician appointments, and reduce long-term health complications.

5. **Advanced analytics applied to patient profiles.** A fifth clinical operations big data lever is applying advanced analytics to patient profiles (e.g., segmentation and predictive modeling) to identify individuals who would benefit from proactive care or lifestyle changes. For instance, these approaches can help identify patients who are at high risk of developing a specific disease (e.g., diabetes) and would benefit from a preventive care program. These approaches can also enable the better selection of patients with a preexisting condition for inclusion in a disease-management program that best matches their needs. And, of course, patient data can provide an enhanced ability to measure the success of these programs, an exercise that poses a major challenge for many current preventive care programs.

Payment/pricing

The two levers in this category mainly involve improving health care payment and pricing, and they focus primarily on payors' operations. Together, they have the potential to create $50 billion in value, half of which would result in cost savings to national health care expenditure.

1. **Automated systems.** The first lever is implementing automated systems (e.g., machine learning techniques such as neural networks) for fraud detection and checking the accuracy and consistency of payors' claims. The US payor industry estimates that 2 to 4 percent of annual claims are fraudulent or unjustified; official estimates for Medicare and Medicaid range up to a 10 percent share. Savings can be achieved through a comprehensive and consistent claims database (e.g., the proposed all-payors claims database) and trained algorithms to process and check claims for accuracy and to detect cases with a high likelihood of fraud, defects, or inaccuracy either retroactively or in real time. When used in near real time, these automated systems can identify overpayments before payouts are made, recouping significant costs.

2. **Health Economics and Outcomes Research and performance-based pricing plans.** The second lever is utilizing Health Economics and Outcomes Research and performance-based pricing plans based on real-world patient outcomes data to arrive at fair economic compensation, from drug prices paid to pharmaceutical companies to reimbursements paid to providers by payors.

   In the case of drug pricing, pharmaceutical companies would share part of the therapeutic risk. For payors, a key benefit is that cost- and risk-sharing schemes for new drugs enable controls or a cap on a significant part of health care spending. At the same time, PMP companies could gain better market access in the presence of strong efforts to contain health care costs. PMP companies can also secure potentially higher revenue from more efficient drug use through innovative pricing schemes. Patients would obtain improved health outcomes with a value-based formulary and gain access to innovative drugs at reasonable costs. To achieve maximum value for the health care system, the United States would need to allow collective bargaining by payors.

Several pharmaceutical pricing pilot programs based on Health Economics and Outcomes Research are in place, primarily in Europe. Novartis, for example, agreed with German health insurers to cover costs in excess of €315 million ($468 million) per year for Lucentis, its drug for treating age-related macular degeneration.

Some payors are also measuring the costs and quality of providers and negotiating reimbursements based on the data. For example, payors may exclude providers whose costs to treat different diseases are out of line after adjusting for comorbidities (the presence of one or more diseases in addition to a primary disease). Alternatively, they may negotiate innovative pricing plans, such as outcome-based payments, if providers achieve specific quality and outcomes benchmarks.

R&D

Five big data levers could improve R&D productivity in the PMP subsector. Together, these levers could create more than $100 billion in value, about $25 billion of which could be in the form of lower national health care expenditure.

1. **Predictive modeling.** The first lever is the aggregation of research data so that PMP companies can perform predictive modeling for new drugs and determine the most efficient and cost-effective allocation of R&D resources. This "rational drug design" means using simulations and modeling based on preclinical or early clinical datasets along the R&D value chain to predict clinical outcomes as promptly as possible. The evaluation factors can include product safety, efficacy, potential side effects, and overall trial outcomes. This predictive modeling can reduce costs by suspending research and expensive clinical trials on suboptimal compounds earlier in the research cycle.

   The benefits of this lever for the PMP sector include lower R&D costs and earlier revenue from a leaner, faster, and more targeted R&D pipeline. The lever helps to bring drugs to market faster and produce more targeted compounds with a higher potential market and therapeutic success rate. Predictive modeling can shave 3 to 5 years off the approximately 13 years it can take to bring a new compound to market.

2. **Statistical tools and algorithms to improve clinical trial design.** Another lever is using statistical tools and algorithms to improve the design of clinical trials and the targeting of patient recruitment in the clinical phases of the R&D process. This lever includes mining patient data to expedite clinical trials by assessing patient recruitment feasibility, recommending more effective protocol designs, and suggesting trial sites with large numbers of potentially eligible patients and strong track records. The techniques that can be employed include performing scenario simulations and modeling to optimize label size (the range of indications applicable to a given drug) to increase the probability of trial success rates. Algorithms can combine R&D and trial data with commercial modeling and historic regulatory data to find the optimal trade-off between the size and characteristics of a targeted patient population for trials and the chances of regulatory approval of the new compound. Analyses can also improve the process of selecting investigators by targeting those with proven performance records.

3. **Analyzing clinical trials data.** A third R&D-related lever is analyzing clinical trials data and patient records to identify additional indications and discover adverse effects. Drug repositioning, or marketing for additional indications, may be

possible after the statistical analysis of large outcome datasets to detect signals of additional benefits. Analyzing the (near) real-time collection of adverse case reports enables pharmacovigilance, surfacing safety signals too rare to appear in a typical clinical trial or, in some cases, identifying events that were hinted at in the clinical trials but that did not have sufficient statistical power.

These analytical programs can be particularly important in the current context in which annual drug withdrawals hit an all-time high in 2008 and the overall number of new drug approvals has been declining. Drug withdrawals are often very publicly damaging to a company. The 2004 removal of the painkiller Vioxx from the market resulted in around $7 billion in legal and claims costs for Merck and a 33 percent drop in shareholder value within just a few days.

4. **Personalized medicine.** Another promising big data innovation that could produce value in the R&D arena is the analysis of emerging large datasets (e.g., genome data) to improve R&D productivity and develop personalized medicine. The objective of this lever is to examine the relationships among genetic variation, predisposition for specific diseases, and specific drug responses and then to account for the genetic variability of individuals in the drug development process.

   Personalized medicine holds the promise of improving health care in three main ways: offering early detection and diagnosis before a patient develops disease symptoms; more effective therapies because patients with the same diagnosis can be segmented according to molecular signature matching (i.e., patients with the same disease often don't respond in the same way to the same therapy, partly because of genetic variation); and the adjustment of drug dosages according to a patient's molecular profile to minimize side effects and maximize response.

   Personalized medicine is in the early stages of development. Impressive initial successes have been reported, particularly in the early detection of breast cancer, in prenatal gene testing, and with dosage testing in the treatment of leukemia and colorectal cancers. We estimate that the potential for cost savings by reducing the prescription of drugs to which individual patients do not respond could be 30 to 70 percent of total cost in some cases. Likewise, earlier detection and treatment could significantly lower the burden of lung cancer on health systems, given that early-stage surgery costs are approximately half those of late-stage treatment.

5. **Analyzing disease patterns.** The fifth R&D-related big data value creation lever is analyzing disease patterns and trends to model future demand and costs and make strategic R&D investment decisions. This analysis can help PMP companies optimize the focus of their R&D as well as the allocation of resources including equipment and staff.

New business models

The proliferation of digital health care data, from clinical to claims information, is creating business models that can complement, or compete with, existing ones and their levers. We highlight two potential new business models:

1. **Aggregating and synthesizing patient clinical records and claims datasets.** The first type of new business model is one that aggregates and analyzes patient records to provide data and services to third parties. Companies could build robust clinical datasets that would enable a number of adjacent businesses. These might include licensing and analyzing clinical outcomes data for payors and regulators to improve clinical decision making, leveraging patient databases

to help PMP companies identify patients meeting certain criteria for inclusion in a clinical trial, or providing access to clinical databases for the discovery of biomarkers that help guide the selection of treatments. An adjacent market that is developing not only provides services based on patient clinical records but also integrates claims datasets to provide services to the PMP sector for R&D and commercial modeling. Clinical and claims data and services markets are just beginning to develop and grow—the rate of their expansion will depend on how rapidly the health care industry implements electronic medical records and evidence-based medicine.

2. **Online platforms and communities.** Another potential new business model enabled by big data is that of online platforms and communities, which are already generating valuable data. Examples of this business model in practice include Web sites such as PatientsLikeMe.com, where individuals can share their experience as patients in the system; Sermo.com, a forum for physicians to share their medical insights; and Participatorymedicine.org, a Web site made available by a nonprofit organization that encourages patient activism. These online platforms could become a valuable source of data. For example, Sermo charges the PMP sector for access to its member physicians and information from their interactions on the site.

Public health

The use of big data can improve public health surveillance and response. By using a nationwide patient and treatment database, public health officials can ensure the rapid, coordinated detection of infectious diseases and a comprehensive outbreak surveillance and response through an Integrated Disease Surveillance and Response program. This lever offers numerous benefits, including a smaller number of claims and payouts, thanks to a timely public health response that would result in a lower incidence of infection. The United States would also be better prepared—in terms of laboratory capacity, for instance—for emerging diseases and outbreaks. There would also be a greater public awareness of the health risks related to infectious diseases, which, in turn, would lower the chance of infections thanks to accurate and timely public health advisories. Taken together, all these components would help to produce a better quality of life.

BIG DATA CAN ENABLE MORE THAN $300 BILLION A YEAR IN VALUE CREATION IN US HEALTH CARE

All the big-data-enabled levers that we have described can play a substantial part in overhauling the productivity of the US health care system, improving the quality of care and treatment, enhancing patients' experience, boosting industry competitiveness, and creating a range of fresh business models and services. In total, we estimate that US health care could capture more than $300 billion in value every year, with two-thirds of that in the form of reductions to national health care expenditure of around 8 percent. Holding health care outcomes constant (a conservative assumption considering that many of the levers will improve health care quality, which is difficult to quantify), accounting for annual operating costs and assuming that the value potential of each big data lever grows linearly with health care expenditure, this would mean that the annual productivity of the US health care sector could grow by an additional 0.7 percent. This productivity boost assumes that the industry realizes all of the potential benefits from the use of big data over the next ten years (Exhibit 15).[43] As we have said, the actual amount of value that the sector will

---

43 This calculation factors in the ongoing operating costs of EMR across the nation, estimated at around $20 billion a year, after initial deployment (estimated at up to $200 billion). See the appendix for our productivity calculation.

capture will depend on the collective actions of health care organizations and policy makers in overcoming structural and other barriers.

The benefits of these dramatic potential improvements would flow to patients, providers, payors, and the PMP sector. However, using these levers would also redistribute value among players throughout the industry as revenue and profits shift and new, imaginative leaders emerge.

Exhibit 15

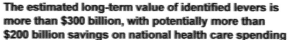

The estimated long-term value of identified levers is more than $300 billion, with potentially more than $200 billion savings on national health care spending

Value potential from use of big data
$ billion per year

▨ Direct reduction on national health care expenditure
▧ Unclear impact on national health care expenditure

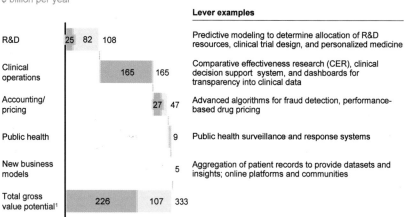

			Lever examples
R&D	25	82	108	Predictive modeling to determine allocation of R&D resources, clinical trial design, and personalized medicine
Clinical operations		165	165	Comparative effectiveness research (CER), clinical decision support system, and dashboards for transparency into clinical data
Accounting/ pricing			27	47	Advanced algorithms for fraud detection, performance-based drug pricing
Public health				9	Public health surveillance and response systems
New business models				5	Aggregation of patient records to provide datasets and insights; online platforms and communities
Total gross value potential[1]	226	107	333	

1 Excluding initial IT investments (~$120 billion–$200 billion) and annual operating costs (~$20 billion per annum).
SOURCE: Expert interviews; press and literature search; McKinsey Global Institute analysis

---

Patients would see lower costs for better care and have broader, clearer access to a wider variety of health care information, making them more informed consumers of the medical system. Patients would be able to compare not only the prices of drugs, treatments, and physicians but also their relative effectiveness, enabling them to choose more effective, better-targeted medicines, many customized to their personal genetic and molecular makeup. Patients would also have access to a wider range of information on epidemics and other public health information crucial to their well-being.

Providers, payors, and the PMP sector will experience a different set of benefits from deploying big data levers. They need to be alert to resulting value shifts and changing business models. Some levers should bring additional value to all stakeholders. For example, by preventing adverse drug events, clinical decision support systems should lead to fewer liability claims for payors, lower malpractice insurance rates for providers, and better outcomes for patients. However, in the case of other levers, one player might gain at the expense of another, a result that would ripple throughout the industry, creating winners and losers at the bottom line. In the case of the adoption of comparative effectiveness research, for instance, providers could see a reduction in their revenue for treatments that are found not to be optimally effective. Remote patient monitoring is another example. This lever will reduce errors and adverse treatment effects and will improve the quality of care and life for those with chronic illnesses. But it will do this by reducing the need for treatment at general hospitals and by cutting adverse drug events, eroding some traditional sources of revenue for hospitals and clinics.

The potential for reduced revenue may prove to be an incentive for hospitals and clinics to look for ways to participate in the wave of new business models and opportunities that big data levers are helping to create. These organizations may, for instance, try to analyze and use patient databases to expand their preventive care offerings. Entirely new business models will, of course, emerge, too. For example, personal health records offered by Google Health and Microsoft Healthvault allow consumers to create personal health profiles and goals, track treatments and prescriptions, and monitor their experiences as patients.

BIG DATA HAVE SIGNIFICANT IMPLICATIONS FOR HEALTH CARE EXECUTIVES AND POLICY MAKERS

It is widely recognized that the health reimbursement plans used in the United States provide little incentive to identify waste, address known operational inefficiencies, or improve productivity. These plans are based on payments for activities, including diagnostic tests, drug prescriptions, physician visits, and procedures ordered, rather than proven health outcomes. They reward a high volume of activity rather than the quality, efficiency, or even necessity of that activity.

Moving toward performance- and outcome-driven reimbursement models will help to align incentives that can help drive the adoption of these levers. Payors and their customers can drive such change, enabled by regulators. The US Department of Veterans Affairs and agencies in the United Kingdom, Italy, and Germany, among others, are working on programs that base payment on effectiveness and patient outcomes. Improving the quality and availability of information on comparisons of treatments, drugs, physicians, and hospitals will help shift this model. Some efforts already exist to rate hospitals and doctors and to create transparency about the cost of different services, and these initiatives are gaining some traction with the public and employers. But all of these results-oriented incentives will have to become embedded and widely accepted in US health care if the big data levers we have discussed are to become an integral part of the system and if their value is to be fully accessed.

It is clear that appropriately aligned incentives can push stakeholders to embrace big data levers to improve performance. The pharmaceutical industry is an obvious example. The industry began mining and aggregating sales and prescription data because this lever helped companies improve their bottom line by more effectively targeting sales, managing sales force resources, and selecting prime areas for R&D.

At the same time, providers will have to invest significantly in deploying electronic medical record systems, which provide a foundation for doing comparative effectiveness research into treatments and drugs. Some estimates put that cost at $80,000 to $100,000 per bed.[44] Although providers will benefit considerably from using such systems (e.g., time savings from pulling and maintaining paper charts), the primary savings will accrue to payors and patients from the identification of the most effective treatments and fewer adverse drug effects. Again, financial incentives would have to be realigned—perhaps through government intervention—before nationwide adoption of electronic medical records and health care information technology will happen.

In addition to structural issues, health care executives will need to overcome challenges related to technology, data access, talent, and changing mind-sets and behaviors to capture value from big data. Technology requirements will vary widely among subsectors

---

44 Francois M. Laflamme, Wayne E. Pietraszek, and Nilesh V. Rajadhyax, "Reforming hospitals with IT investment," *McKinsey Quarterly*, August 2010.

and organizations. For instance, significant capital investments will frequently be required to modernize and standardize IT systems and make them compatible to optimize the value creation that can be gleaned from big data. To date, meaningful adoption of electronic medical records continues to run at around 20 percent; the availability of federal incentives could help to boost that rate.[45] For many providers, putting the technology in place to generate and capture digital clinical data is the key first step. This will be a formidable challenge in itself because large-scale IT projects are notoriously difficult to execute.[46] An equally important task is to ensure that interoperable standards are in place so that data generated at one provider can be accessed in a useful form by another.

For more sophisticated PMP companies, the big data technology enhancements required may involve the provision of sufficient storage or the implementation of advanced analytics. For others, the technology challenges will include consolidating fragmented internal databases and making them consistent with one another in a format that will allow an integrated view of information to be available as needed. In many organizations, the internal accessibility and availability of various databases remains severely limited.

The power of many of the big data levers we've described depends on access to data—and often at a scale beyond those that an individual organization generates. These levers may require combining disparate sets of data such as patient records and clinical claims data. Stakeholders in the industry do not often share existing datasets, because of legal constraints such as privacy laws, a lack of incentives, or incompatible IT systems or formats. The sensitive nature of health information, and the potential for discrimination based on it, makes security and privacy rights protection critical. Many countries have regulations such as HIPAA and HITECH, the US laws designed to protect the security and privacy of health records. As using big data becomes more important to the industry, policy makers may have to reevaluate these laws or intervene to ensure that access to data is available in a safe and secure way that also enables health care outcomes to be optimized.

Finally, the difficulties in recruiting and retaining the right talent and forging the right mind-sets within institutions are among the most stubborn obstacles to capturing the value opportunities of big data. Leaders who understand what types of valuable insights can come from data and talent that can analyze large volumes of data are essential. The willingness of employees to use data-driven insights in their decision making is also critical. Capturing the cost savings of comparative effectiveness research, for example, will require physicians to prescribe the most cost-effective interventions according to guidelines derived from big data. But studies in many clinical areas show that physicians often resist, or simply do not comply with, such guidelines. Achieving such a shift will be difficult—but necessary.

---

45 National Center for Health Statistics, Centers for Disease Control and Prevention, "Electronic medical record/electronic health record use by office-based physicians," December 2009; Ashish K. Jha et al., "Use of electronic health records in US hospitals," *New England Journal of Medicine* 360(16), April 16, 2009:1628–38.

46 For more on the challenges of implementing IT successfully in health care providers and payors, see "Debunking the three leading misperceptions about health care IT," *Health International 2010*, Number 10.

□ □ □

The US health care sector faces an urgent imperative to achieve a radical improvement in its cost-effectiveness. Our research shows that a range of levers using big data can be a critical enabler in reducing cost while at least maintaining health care quality. However, the US health care industry will not achieve the significant value available from big data without radical changes in regulations and systemwide incentives. Achieving those changes will be difficult—but the potential prize is so great that health care executives and policy makers should not ignore these opportunities.

3b. Public sector administration (European Union)

Governments in many parts of the world are under increasing pressure to boost their productivity—in other words, do more with less. Particularly in the aftermath of the recent global recession, many governments are faced with having to continue to provide a high level of public services at a time of significant budgetary constraint as they seek to reduce large budget deficits and national debt levels built up when they spent public money heavily to stimulate growth. Beyond the pressures of reducing debt levels, many countries face medium- to long-term budgetary constraints caused by aging populations that will significantly increase demand for medical and social services.

As recent MGI research has shown, the way that governments will need to cope with such constraints is through achieving a step change in their (often relatively low) productivity.[47] While productivity in the public sector is not easy to measure, there is evidence that public sector productivity growth has fallen behind that of the private sector in many (or most) economies. Experimental estimates by the UK Office of National Statistics showed declining productivity in the public sector from 1995 to 2005, while MGI research showed positive productivity growth in the market sector.[48] In large part, the deteriorating productivity performance of the UK public sector was the result of the government's increasing employment.[49]

Can big data help the public sector raise its game on productivity? To attempt to answer this question, we studied the administrative activities of the public sector, with a focus on Europe (see Box 7, "How we studied public sector administration"). We found that big data levers, such as increasing transparency and applying advanced analytics, offer the public sector a powerful arsenal of strategies and techniques for boosting productivity and achieving higher levels of efficiency and effectiveness. Our research shows Europe's public sector could potentially reduce the costs of administrative activities by 15 to 20 percent, creating the equivalent of €150 billion to €300 billion ($223 billion to $446 billion)—or even higher—in new value. This estimate includes both efficiency gains and a reduction in the gap between actual and potential collection of tax revenue. These levers could accelerate annual productivity growth by up to 0.5 percentage points over the next ten years.

We believe that big data can play a similar role in other countries and regions, too. Other governments around the world face many of the same social and economic challenges, and the big data opportunities we discuss in this Europe-focused case study will apply elsewhere, particularly in other developed countries and regions.

47 See Martin N. Baily, Karen Croxson, Thomas Dohrmann, and Lenny Mendonca, *The public sector productivity imperative*, McKinsey & Company, March 2011 (www.mckinsey.com/en/Client_Service/Public_Sector/Latest_thinking/~/media/McKinsey/dotcom/client_service/Public%20Sector/PDFS/Public%20Sector%20Productivity%20Imperative_March%202011.ashx); and Tony Danker, Thomas Dohrmann, Nancy Killefer, and Lenny Mendonca, "How can American government meet its productivity challenge?" *McKinsey Quarterly*, July 2006 (www.mckinseyquarterly.com). Also see MGI reports *Beyond austerity: A path to economic growth and renewal in Europe*, October 2010, and *Growth and renewal in the United States: Retooling America's economic engine*, February 2011 (www.mckinsey.com/.mgi).

48 Note that market sector refers to the private sector plus that part of the public sector that sells goods or services for a fee. Also, it should be noted that public sector productivity figures are experimental, outcome-based (not adjusted for value), and divided by total inputs, while market sector productivity figures are based on value added and labor inputs. Experimental estimates are those made using cutting-edge, and therefore not proven, methodologies.

49 *From austerity to prosperity: Seven priorities for the long term*, McKinsey Global Institute, November 2010 (www.mckinsey.com/mgi).

Box 7. How we studied public sector administration

The public sector offers particular challenges because it is so tremendously diverse in its functions and budgets. We have focused on administration in two common types of government agencies, tax and labor, and then extended our analysis to other relevant parts of the government. Administrative work is arguably the foundation of many public sector functions and agencies, and many aspects of this type of work are common across agencies. Typically, administrative work features many "customer" interactions and generates a high volume of forms and/or payments to process.

The work of tax and labor agencies is a classic example. The main activities of tax agencies include submissions processing, examinations, collections, and taxpayer services, all on a large scale. Labor agencies perform a variety of analytical functions, including examining markets, screening customers, and then distributing appropriate benefits and employment services. Other agencies, including transportation and immigration, have similar functions and responsibilities. Private sector activities including the processing of insurance claims also involve similar administrative tasks, and we can draw additional insights from what we know of these activities in the private sector.

We began by conducting microanalyses of tax and labor agencies in which we identified and estimated the size of the potential value that big levers can create. We then extrapolated these findings to estimate the value potential of those levers in other similar departments. Some of the levers we discovered were specific to the tax and labor agencies, including levers aimed at reducing the tax gap or reducing fraudulent benefit payments. However, many efficiency levers such as performance dashboards and data integration and mashups are relevant for many other agencies, too (see appendix for more detail on our methodology).

THE PUBLIC SECTOR FACES A SIGNIFICANT PERFORMANCE CHALLENGE

Europe's public sector accounts for almost half of GDP, including transfer payments that account for about 20 percent.[50] Excluding transfer payments, about 10 to 30 percent of this share is attributable to administration.[51] This high share of overall economic output puts considerable long-term strain on Europe's budgetary and debt positions—over and above the impact of the recent global recession. Today, levels of public debt are already high, and previous MGI research demonstrates that the process of reducing debt after recessions is a lengthy one.[52]

Compounding the budgetary pressures faced by Europe's government is the continent's aging demographic. By 2025, close to 30 percent of the population in mature economies across the globe will be aged 60 or over, up from 20 percent in 2000. Social security, health, and pensions will all face increasing demand (Exhibit 16).

50 OECD statistical database.

51 Transfer payments redistribute income in the market system. Examples include welfare (financial aid), social security, and government subsidies for certain businesses (firms).

52 *Debt and deleveraging: The global credit bubble and its economic consequences*, McKinsey Global Institute, January 2010 (www.mckinsey.com/mgi).

Exhibit 16

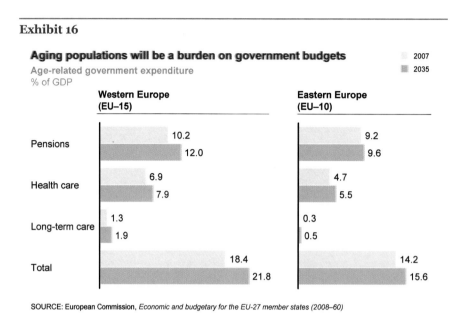

Aging populations will be a burden on government budgets

Age-related government expenditure
% of GDP

2007
2035

	Western Europe (EU–15)	Eastern Europe (EU–10)
Pensions	10.2 / 12.0	9.2 / 9.6
Health care	6.9 / 7.9	4.7 / 5.5
Long-term care	1.3 / 1.9	0.3 / 0.5
Total	18.4 / 21.8	14.2 / 15.6

SOURCE: European Commission, *Economic and budgetary for the EU-27 member states (2008–60)*

WHAT KINDS OF DATA DO PUBLIC SECTOR ADMINISTRATION GENERATE?

Data generated in public sector administration are primarily textual or numerical. So, in comparison with sectors such as the provision of health care that generates substantial amounts of multimedia content (extensive electronic imaging, for instance, in addition to text), we find that public sector administration tends to generate a lower—but still substantial—volume of unique data as measured in bytes. However, in contrast to health care, the vast majority—up to 90 percent—of the data generated in public sector administration is created in digital form, partly as a result of e-government initiatives undertaken during the past 15 years.

However, even in countries whose e-government programs are the most advanced, public sector agencies often do not make data available in an effective manner either across organizational silos or to citizens and businesses. Formatting and input protocols are often inconsistent. Instead of moving data electronically, it is not uncommon for an employee in one agency to receive a faxed copy or mailed CD of data from another agency, even though those data may be stored electronically. And there are some policy and/or legal restrictions that prevent data sharing.

Lack of transparency into government performance data can also be a contributing factor to the productivity challenges mentioned previously. It is difficult to improve activities that aren't measured, and the relative lack of transparency into public sector performance and productivity metrics is a contributing factor to the productivity gap described earlier.

THE PUBLIC SECTOR CAN USE BIG DATA LEVERS IN EACH OF THE FIVE CATEGORIES WE HAVE IDENTIFIED

The public sector in Europe and beyond has the opportunity to deploy big data levers in each of the five broad categories that emerge from our research across sectors. The levers that we discuss apply to tax and labor agencies, but we believe that their use can be just as relevant in other parts of the public sector.

1. Creating transparency

Both external stakeholders such as citizens and businesses and internal stakeholders such as government employees and agencies can improve their efficiency when data from large public sector databases are made more accessible. For example, government agencies regularly collect a large amount of data on individuals and businesses through various regulatory and other filings. Yet citizens and businesses frequently have to fill out forms for which some of the data have already been collected and stored. If agencies were to pre-fill forms for citizens and businesses from data already stored in government databases, this would save time for the submitters of forms as well as government agencies that would not have to re-input data. Pre-filling would also have the advantage of reducing errors and speeding up processing time. Taking this approach would, however, require policy and statutory barriers to sharing data to be overcome.

The Swedish Tax Agency pre-fills forms for its citizens, including income data and the previous year's taxes paid. The agency allows citizens to confirm or change that information using short message service (SMS) by cell phone or Internet. The potential time savings for taxpayers can be significant. In the United States, for instance, individual taxpayers spend an estimated 5 to 20 hours or more on tax filing activities. Pre-filling can also make substantial time savings for tax authorities. One tax authority was able to redeploy about 15 percent of staff assigned to the processing of submissions.

Government employees and their respective agencies can also benefit from making data available across agencies and organizational silos. This can reduce search times between and within agencies, which can make up a significant portion of government employees' time. One tax agency was able to redeploy 20 percent of its full-time employees by gaining online access to a housing transfer deed databases rather than collecting the data from another government agency on physical media (CDs) and manually searching through the data.

Increasingly more governments (at all levels) are beginning to adopt "open data" principles in which they make more raw government databases available to the public. Data.gov.uk in the United Kingdom and the Aporta Web portal in Spain (www. proyectoaporta.es) are central Web sites that are examples of this trend, in which external stakeholders can access more and more large databases. Such efforts have unlocked a tremendous amount of innovation that combines data from multiple sources (e.g., "official" government information from law enforcement and public works with "unofficial" citizen-reported information from social media) to create services such as hyperlocal news that describes events specific to a city block. Other examples, including expectmore.gov and Dr. Foster Intelligence, which provides health care information to UK citizens, are designed to measure program performance directly (see item 5 in this section on new business models for further discussion of these possibilities).

2. Enabling experimentation to discover needs, expose variability, and improve performance

One highly valuable contribution that big data can make is to uncover tremendous variability in performance within different parts of a government agency that are performing broadly similar functions—a variability that doesn't show up at the aggregate level. Such information can be a very valuable opportunity for improving the performance of operating units within an agency. For example, performance dashboards that display operational and financial data allow an agency to measure and compare the performance of its different units and develop approaches to improve productivity. Observers tend to cite a lack of external competition as an explanation for the relatively low productivity in public sector administration, and this

58

certainly plays a part. But even in a context of weak competitive pressure, the ability to expose variation in performance among different public sector units can create internal competition that drives performance higher. Even in the absence of tangible financial rewards for improving performance, managers in subpar units will often want to improve on that performance because they feel uncomfortable being shown publicly to be toward the bottom of the agency pile (although they may also work harder to boost performance because this might enhance their chances of promotion and more pay down the line).[53]

Best practice tax agencies use integrated monthly scorecards that measure revenue collected and that track customer satisfaction scores, staff engagement scores, and feedback from the public and agency heads. Elevating the bottom quartile in performance terms by one or two quartiles can be a large opportunity to improve efficiency. While private sector business units can vary in their performance by a factor of two, public sector units can vary by a factor of six.[54] Agencies with counterparts in other countries can extend their comparisons of performance from internal to global benchmarks (Exhibit 17).

Exhibit 17

Tax agencies in different countries vary in their performance levels

Performance scores indexed to 100

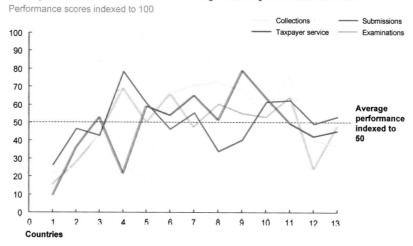

SOURCE: McKinsey tax benchmarking study (includes analysis of 13 countries: Australia, Belgium, Brazil, Canada, Chile, Denmark, France, Ireland, Norway, South Africa, Spain, Sweden, and the United States)

Comparison engines can allow public sector administrators to measure and rank the performance of vendors and service providers. Procurement typically offers a large opportunity for cost savings for government as purchasing accounts on average for about one-third of public sector spending (excluding transfer payments). McKinsey's experience of working on public sector projects suggests that government can, on average, generate savings of up to 30 percent from awarding contracts more effectively across a range of services and goods.[55]

53 Some managers in public sector do receive bonuses for strong performance. For more on using status rewards to motivate good performance, see Timothy Besley and Maitreesh Ghatak, "Status incentives," *American Economic Review* 98(2), 2008: 206–11.

54 McKinsey conducted an in-depth benchmarking of 13 tax agencies globally in 2008 and 2009. For the findings, see Thomas Dohrmann and Gary Pinshaw, *The road to improved compliance*, McKinsey white paper, September 2009.

55 Percent as a basis of procurement cost; see Christian Husted and Nicolas Reinecke, "Improving public-sector purchasing," *McKinsey on Government*, 2009.

Citizens and external stakeholders can also use public sector data that expose variability in performance. In the United Kingdom, the government is making data on health care outcomes available so that citizens can make more informed decisions about providers. In similar fashion, making data available on educational outcomes at primary and secondary schools can allow parents to make more informed decisions about where to live or in which schools to place their children. In addition to arming consumers of such public services with the information they need to make effective choices, making these types of data openly available is likely to incentivize providers of such services to improve their performance.

3. Segmenting populations to customize actions

Using segmentation to tailor services to individuals has long been an accepted practice in the private sector. However, the ethos of the public sector tends to be that governments should provide exactly the same services to all citizens. Our research shows that segmenting and tailoring government services to individuals and population cohorts can increase effectiveness, efficiency, and citizen satisfaction. For example, Bundesagentur für Arbeit (German Federal Labor Agency, or BA for short) analyzed its huge amount of historical data on its customers, including histories of unemployed workers, the interventions that it took, and outcomes including data on how long it took people to find a job. The idea was to develop a segmentation based on this analysis so that the agency could tailor its interventions for unemployed workers. This process, along with other initiatives applied over three years, allowed the agency to reduce its spending by €10 billion ($14.9 billion) annually at the same time as cutting the amount of time that unemployed workers took to find employment, and increasing the satisfaction among users of its services (see Box 8, "Germany's federal labor agency has used big data to cut significant cost from its operations").

Similarly, best practice tax agencies are using big data to segment individual and business taxpayers, separating them into categories and classes for examination and collection activities. For example, these agencies can categorize taxpayers by geography, their compliance history, potential risk of default, collection difficulty, and, of course, income level and demographics. Using effective segmentation can help close the gap between actual and potential collections by up to 10 percent. At the same time, more targeted interactions can increase customer satisfaction by as much as 15 percent.

4. Replacing/supporting human decision making with automated algorithms

Some of the more sophisticated applications of big data use automated algorithms to analyze large datasets in order to help make better decisions. These types of techniques can often be very effectively applied in compliance activities, for example, among public sector agencies that need to find anomalies in payments such as in tax collections or benefit payments from labor or social security departments. Sophisticated tax agencies apply automated algorithms that perform systematic, multilevel checks on tax returns and automatically flag returns that require further examination or auditing. This approach can improve collections considerably, reducing the tax gap by up to 10 percentage points. Similar methods can be used by other agencies to play an effective role in counterterrorism and child protection.

Algorithms can crawl through big data from a variety of sources, identifying inconsistencies, errors, and fraud. For instance, rule-based algorithms can flag suspicious correlations such as a person receiving unemployment benefits while filing for a work-related accident. Using more sophisticated and well-tuned algorithmic techniques such as neural networks can reduce the probability of both false positives (selecting an item for further examination that does not have an issue) and false negatives (not selecting an item for further examination where there is an issue). After using automated analyses, BA reported a 20 percent reduction in erroneously paid benefits.

Box 8. Germany's federal labor agency has used big data to cut significant cost from its operations

The Bundesagentur für Arbeit (German Federal Labor Agency, or BA for short), with a €54 billion annual budget and 120,000 full-time employees, has sharply improved its customer services and cut around €10 billion of costs in recent years by using big data strategies (Exhibit 18). BA finds jobs for the unemployed and provides a full range of counseling and support services through ten regional centers and 178 employment agencies.

The agency built capabilities for producing and analyzing data that enabled a range of new programs and new approaches to existing programs. BA is now able to analyze outcomes data for its placement programs more accurately, spotting those programs that are relatively ineffective and improving or eliminating them. The agency has greatly refined its ability to define and evaluate the characteristics of its unemployed and partially employed customers. As a result, BA has developed a segmented approach that helps the agency offer more effective placement and counseling to more carefully targeted customer segments. Surveys of their customers show that they perceive and highly approve of the changes BA is making.

Exhibit 18

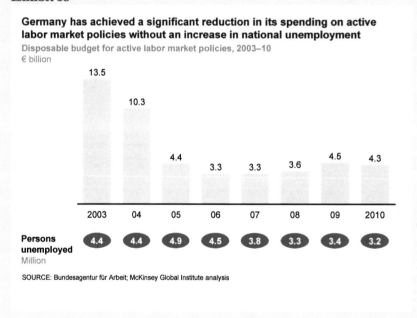

Germany has achieved a significant reduction in its spending on active labor market policies without an increase in national unemployment

Disposable budget for active labor market policies, 2003–10
€ billion

2003	04	05	06	07	08	09	2010
13.5	10.3	4.4	3.3	3.3	3.6	4.5	4.3

Persons unemployed
Million

| 4.4 | 4.4 | 4.9 | 4.5 | 3.8 | 3.3 | 3.4 | 3.2 |

SOURCE: Bundesagentur für Arbeit; McKinsey Global Institute analysis

5. Innovating new business models, products, and services with big data

Big data from government can unlock innovation both inside and outside the public sector. Providing readily accessible big data tools and analytics can allow commercial, nonprofit, and individual third parties to create new value for the public sector in a variety of ways. These could include feedback on services, insight into better management practices, and suggestions for improving new and existing programs. Big data innovation can lead to experiments in public policy and public sector programs to improve government performance. In the United Kingdom, for instance, the nonprofit Open Knowledge

Foundation used databases made available through the government's open data initiative to develop wheredoesmymoneygo.org, a site that makes it easier for citizens to view and understand UK public spending through analysis and visualization of the data.[56]

The startup company BrightScope mined data from the US Department of Labor about 401(k) management fees paid by employers and discovered that small businesses were paying in excess of $4 billion more in management fees than bigger companies. Based on those data, and data from a few public sources such as the Securities and Exchange Commission and the US Census Bureau, BrightScope now provides an online tool to rate 401(k) plans quantitatively.

In April 2011, a consortium of European open data organizations announced an "open data challenge," a contest for designers, developers, researchers, and the general public to come up with ideas, applications, visualizations, and derived datasets based on datasets produced by European public bodies. The consortium made €20,000 in prize money available. This project was partly inspired by the District of Columbia's Apps for Democracy contest, which attracted more than 40 successful applications worth at least $2 million to the DC municipal government at a total cost of $50,000.

As in the other industry and business sectors we studied, significant value can be captured merely by making data available and transparent (and applying simple analytics). Potential gains increase sharply as stakeholders move to advanced analytics techniques such as applying complex algorithms and segmentation techniques.

THE POTENTIAL BENEFITS OF BIG DATA IN PUBLIC SECTOR ADMINISTRATION

Across Europe's public sector, the big data levers we identified for administration can bring three main categories of quantifiable monetary value as long as the right policies and enablers are in place. These are cost savings from operational efficiency, a reduction in the cost of errors and fraud in benefit administration, and an increase in tax receipts by narrowing the tax gap. We estimate that the efficiency levers we have identified apply to 20 to 25 percent of operating budgets with potential savings of 15 to 20 percent. Reducing error and the cost of benefits received fraudulently is possible in an estimated 1 to 3 percent of transfer payments (note that this accounts for the portion of transfer payments that have nonnegligible amounts of error and fraud and the estimated percentage cost of error and fraud), saving up to 40 percent of the cost incurred from these sources.[57] With respect to increasing tax receipts, we estimate the tax gap to be in the range of 5 to 10 percent of total European tax receipts and that up to 20 percent of that can be recouped. Altogether, the public sectors of Europe's 23 largest governments could potentially create €150 billion to €300 billion—and potentially more—in new value annually over ten years. This implies boosting annual productivity growth rates in the public sector by about 0.5 percentage points above those expected, if current trends hold (Exhibit 19).

56 See Jason Baumgarten and Michael Chui, "E-government 2.0," *McKinsey Quarterly*, July 2009 for a story about the Sunlight Foundation, an organization that created a similar site in the United States.

57 Based on studies done by governments, we estimate that fraud or error can affect approximately 55 percent of transfer payments and that this error and fraud can boost costs by up to 3 percent.

Exhibit 19

Big data has the potential to create €150 billion to €300 billion or more in value across the OECD-Europe public sector

		Total base[1] € billion	Addressable %	Reduction %	Total value € billion
Operational efficiency savings	Operating expenditure	4,000	20–25	15–20	120–200
Reduction in fraud and error	Transfer payment	2,500	1–3[2]	30–40	7–30
Increase in tax collection	Tax revenue	5,400	5–10[3]	10–20	25–110
					150–300+

1 Base for operational efficiency savings is total government expenditure net of transfer payments; base for reduction in fraud is total government transfer payments; base for increase in tax collection is tax revenue.
2 Takes into account the percentage of transfer payment that can have fraud/error as well as the estimated cost of error and fraud.
3 In the case of tax collection, the percentage addressable refers to the percentage estimated tax gap.
NOTE: Numbers may not sum due to rounding.
SOURCE: International Monetary Fund; OECD; McKinsey Global Institute analysis

In addition, big data can deliver a range of substantial nonmonetary gains in the public sector, including the improved allocation of funding into programs, higher-quality services, increased public sector accountability, a better-informed citizenry, and almost certainly enhanced public trust in government.[58] After one of the EU labor agencies began segmenting its services, there was a documented increase in the quality of interaction between the agency's customers and case managers. Citizens and business can spend less time and effort in their interactions with government agencies and receive services better targeted to their needs. Greater transparency of information creates improved accountability in public sector agencies and improved public trust. Dashboards and comparative engines offer citizens the means of measuring the effectiveness of programs and policies. One of the hidden benefits of making citizens' own data available to them is that they are usually the most motivated to ensure that those records are accurate. So giving citizens the ability to correct erroneous personal information in agency databases electronically can improve the accuracy of government databases. All of the levers we have discussed can lead to more informed and better decisions by citizens, policy makers, and public sector executives.

PUBLIC SECTOR LEADERS NEED TO ADDRESS A RANGE OF ISSUES TO USE BIG DATA EFFECTIVELY

Public sector leaders who want to realize the value potential offered by big data need to address a number of internal and external issues. These include implementing appropriate technology, recruiting and training talented personnel, and managing change within their organizations. Just as important, government will need to use policy to support the capture of value from big data and the sharing of data across agencies.

The first task is to establish a culture within the public sector in which decisions aimed at improving performance are made on the basis of data. Only when the government makes its performance goals and supporting data transparent will government agencies and the public engage more meaningfully in those objectives. When the

---

58 These improvements in the quality of government services provided were not included in the productivity calculation.

government establishes institutions to review its accountability and productivity, citizens and public sector employees "get the message."

Fortunately, many of the data in the public sector administrative functions of developed countries are already in digital form, but agencies vary significantly in the sophistication with which they handle that digital information.[59] Some agencies will still need to deal with issues such as inconsistent data formats and definitions, and problems associated with legacy systems. The ability to integrate different datasets will be critical to, for example, enabling tax agencies to pre-fill taxpayers' forms and screen them automatically, and labor agencies to accurately integrate data on the unemployed so that they can target services more efficiently. Anecdotally, tax agencies in Europe and in other regions report difficulties in obtaining and using data from other agencies because of incompatible data formats.

Recruiting and retaining analytical talent will be a critical issue for public sector agencies, just as it is in the private sector. Arguably the analytical talent gap will be even greater in the public sector, given its lackluster track record of competing for top talent, and it is vital that public sector leaders understand the need to tackle this shortfall. There will also be increasing demand for personnel who can effectively manage and adapt to change, and some governments will need to overcome a culture in which seniority reigns and blunts the impact of incentives for better performance. The public sector needs to change the attitude of employees toward data sharing and use, offering appropriate incentives and systems to ensure that the insights derived from big data actually drive the actions and decisions in organizations. The mind-set of employees can be as great a barrier to realizing value from big data as technological inadequacy.

In the area of balancing privacy rights and data access, action across departments is likely to be helpful. New laws or regulations may be necessary to enable government agencies to access data from their counterparts in other parts of the system while protecting the security of that information and privacy of its subjects. Policy makers need to make decisions on privacy in conjunction with public opinion, informing citizens about the trade-offs between the privacy and security risks of sharing data and the benefits of sharing data.

□ □ □

The public sector in advanced economies is facing unprecedented pressures to improve productivity, and our analysis of public administration in Europe demonstrates that big data levers can make a significant contribution to this effort around the world. Using big data intelligently has the potential to generate significant value for the public sector as long as action is taken to overcome technological barriers, to recruit and retrain people with the appropriate skills, and to manage the changes needed within organizations to embrace and leverage big data.

---

59 This observation refers to the government administrative functions studied in this deep dive, which did not include education or government-run health care. For much of Europe, online delivery of public services has made steady progress. The most basic 20 eServices (including online tax returns and school enrollments) stood at an average availability of 82 percent across Europe in 2010. For more, see *Digitizing public services in Europe: Putting ambition to action*, European Commission, December 2010.

3c. Retail (United States)

In the US retail industry, the use of information technology and digital data has been instrumental in boosting the profitability of individual players and the productivity of the entire sector for decades. In the coming years, the continued adoption and development of big data levers have the potential to further increase sector-wide productivity by at least 0.5 percent a year through 2020. Among individual firms, these levers could increase operating margins by more than 60 percent for those pioneers that maximize their use of big data. Such a boost in profitability would be especially significant in a sector where margins are notoriously tight. This is also a rich domain in which to examine interactions between retailers and consumers. This is an area in which digital data are playing an increasing role as consumers search, research, compare, buy, and obtain support online, and the products sold by retailers increasingly generate their own digital data. Of course, the value that players in the retail sector and their customers will actually capture will depend critically on the actions of retailers to overcome barriers related to technology, talent, and organizational culture.

This study focuses on the US retail sector, but we also draw on the best practices and experiences of companies around the world. The potential positive impact from the majority of the big data levers we describe would almost certainly be similar in other developed nations. We examined the application of big data in the majority of retail subsectors as described by the standard North American Industry Classification System (NAICS). Specifically, we include in our analysis those subsectors in which customers make small- to moderate-sized average individual purchases and those with a moderate to high frequency of interaction (see Box 9, "Which retail subsectors did we study?"). We do not include the private-label businesses of retailers. We cover suppliers of goods in our case study on manufacturing.

Box 9. Which retail subsectors did we study?

We looked at 10 of the 12 NAICS retail subsectors for our analysis: health and personal care; general merchandise; building materials and garden equipment; nonstore retailers; food and beverage; clothing and accessories; sporting goods, hobby, book, and music; electronics and appliances; miscellaneous; and furniture and home furnishings.

We did not include motor vehicle and parts dealers or gas stations. The primary reason for excluding motor vehicle dealers was that the frequency of purchases of motor vehicles, often the second-most valuable item in a household after a home itself, is relatively rare, so the level of interactions with consumers is also at a different scale and frequency compared with other retail subsectors. We chose not to cover gas stations because the sale of a commodity (gasoline) makes it less comparable to other retail subsectors with far more variety in products and whose input costs are less dominated by a single volatile factor (oil prices).

RETAIL IS AN IMPORTANT COMPONENT OF THE US ECONOMY, BUT PROFITABILITY IS UNDER INTENSE PRESSURE

Retail makes up a sizable part of the US economy. In 2009, that share was an estimated 6 percent of the economy, down a percentage point from 2000. Industry forecasts point to only modest growth over the next five years as the sector steadily, but slowly, recovers from recession. Historical trends have demonstrated that there is a close relationship between growth in retail and that of developed market economies as a whole. As a matter of reference, the International Monetary Fund (IMF) is predicting annual US GDP growth of 2.7 percent through 2015.

Retail's share of overall consumer spending has been in decline, falling from 50 percent in 1990 to 42 percent in 2009. And the sector's profitability is under intense pressure, squeezed both by suppliers, who have been capturing an increasing amount of surplus, and by customers, who are putting pressure on prices. For every $1.00 of operating profit on consumer goods in 2008, retailers collected approximately $0.31, down from $0.60 in 1999, while suppliers, packagers, and others below retail on the value chain received $0.69 (Exhibit 20).

Exhibit 20

Downward pricing pressure on retailers from suppliers has squeezed retailers' portion of the consumer profit pool

Operating profit pool for consumer goods
%

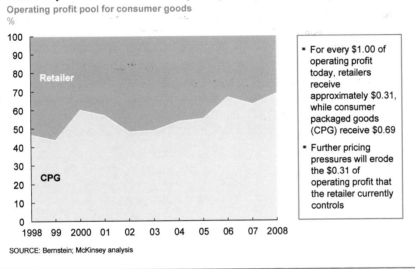

SOURCE: Bernstein; McKinsey analysis

A number of big data developments will put more downward pricing pressure on retailers. This squeeze will come from a variety of new technologies that give shoppers powerful pricing, promotional, and product information, frequently in real time. Applications such as RedLaser, for instance, let shoppers scan the bar code of an item in-store with their smartphones and obtain immediate price and product comparisons. In addition, the adoption of online and mobile commerce (more than 50 percent of retail sales will be online or influenced by online channels by 2014) could provide a huge increase in price transparency that will shift immense value to consumers (Exhibit 21). This trend is likely to erode margins for retailers that are competing solely on price. It is already clear that where shoppers have easy access to cross-retailer price comparisons, prices tend to be materially lower.[60]

---

60 There is a long history of academic literature on the relationship between advertising (online and offline) and prices that has covered products from eyeglasses to alcohol and services such as attorneys. See, for example, Lee Benham, "The effect of advertising on the price of eyeglasses," *Journal of Law and Economics* 15(2), October 1972: 337–52.

66

Exhibit 21

US online and Web-influenced retail sales are forecast to become more than half of all sales by 2013

$ billion

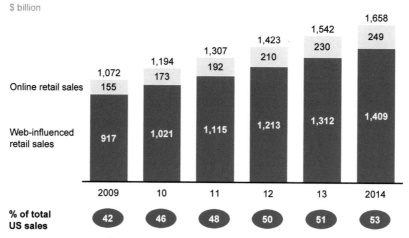

SOURCE: Forrester Research Web-influenced retail sales forecast, December 2009

INFORMATION TECHNOLOGY TRENDS OFFER SIGNIFICANT NEW OPPORTUNITIES TO CREATE VALUE IN RETAIL

While big data linked to new technology does squeeze the industry in some ways, it also offers significant new opportunities for creating value. Sector retailers and their competitors are in a constant race to identify and implement those big data levers that will give them an edge in the market. The volume of data is growing inexorably as retailers not only record every customer transaction and operation but also keep track of emerging data sources such as radio-frequency identification (RFID) chips that track products, and online customer behavior and sentiment.

In fact, US retail has been leveraging information technology for decades. Point-of-sale transactional data, primarily obtained from the use of bar codes, first appeared in the 1970s.[61] Since the 1990s, many leading retailers have been using store-level and supply chain data to optimize distribution and logistics, sharpen merchandise planning and management, and upgrade store operations. In previous MGI research on the acceleration of productivity in general merchandise retail in the 1990s, we found that Wal-Mart directly and indirectly caused the bulk of the productivity acceleration through ongoing managerial innovation (e.g., big-box formats, everyday low price) that increased competitive intensity and drove the diffusion of managerial and technological best practices.[62] Wal-Mart pioneered the expansion of an electronic data interchange system to connect its supply chain electronically. Wal-Mart also developed "Retail Link," a tool that gives its suppliers a view of demand in its stores so that they know when stores should be restocked rather than waiting for an order from Wal-Mart. This "vendor-managed inventory" was a revolutionary concept when it was introduced in the late 1980s. Both of these initiatives improved the

61 A package of Wrigley's chewing gum was the first grocery item scanned using Universal Product Code—in a Marsh Supermarket in Troy, Ohio, in 1974.

62 For more on drivers of productivity, in particular technology in the retail sector in the 1990s, see *How IT enables productivity growth*, McKinsey Global Institute, November 2002 (www.mckinsey.com/mgi).

retailer's capital and labor productivity and cost position. When other retailers moved in the 1990s to emulate what Wal-Mart had pioneered in order to remain competitive, productivity surged across the industry.

Today, leading players are mining customer data to inform decisions they make about managing their supply chain to merchandising and pricing. Wal-Mart's detailed and cost-efficient customer tracking gives the retailer the ability to mine petabytes of data on customer preferences and buying behavior, and thereby win important pricing and distribution concessions from consumer product goods companies. Retailers across the industry are becoming more sophisticated in slicing and dicing big data they collect from multiple sales channels, catalogs, stores, and online interactions. The widespread use of increasingly granular customer data can enable retailers to improve the effectiveness of their marketing and merchandising. Big data levers applied to operations and supply chains will continue to reduce costs and increasingly create new competitive advantages and strategies for growing retailers' revenue.

MGI HAS IDENTIFIED 16 BIG DATA LEVERS IN RETAIL

We have identified 16 big data retail levers that retailers can employ along the value chain. These levers fall into in the five main categories of marketing, merchandising, operations, supply chain, and new business models (Exhibit 22).

Exhibit 22

Big data retail levers can be grouped by function

Function	Big data lever
Marketing	▪ Cross-selling ▪ Location based marketing ▪ In-store behavior analysis ▪ Customer micro-segmentation ▪ Sentiment analysis ▪ Enhancing the multichannel consumer experience
Merchandising	▪ Assortment optimization ▪ Pricing optimization ▪ Placement and design optimization
Operations	▪ Performance transparency ▪ Labor inputs optimization
Supply chain	▪ Inventory management ▪ Distribution and logistics optimization ▪ Informing supplier negotiations
New business models	▪ Price comparison services ▪ Web-based markets

SOURCE: McKinsey Global Institute analysis

Marketing

1. **Cross-selling.** State-of-the-art cross-selling uses all the data that can be known about a customer, including the customer's demographics, purchase history, preferences, real-time locations, and other facts to increase the average purchase size. For example, Amazon.com employs collaborative filtering to generate "you might also want" prompts for each product bought or visited. At one point, Amazon reported that 30 percent of sales were due to its recommendation engine. Another example of this lever is using big data analyses to optimize in-store promotions that link complementary items and bundled products.

2. **Location-based marketing.** Location-based marketing relies on the growing adoption of smartphones and other personal location data-enabled mobile devices. It targets consumers who are close to stores or already in them. For instance, as a consumer approaches an apparel store, that store may send a special offer on a sweater to the customer's smartphone. The startup PlaceCast claims that more than 50 percent of its users have made a purchase as a result of such location-based ads. Nearly 50 percent of smartphone owners use or plan to use their phones for mobile shopping.[63]

3. **In-store behavior analysis.** Analyzing data on in-store behavior can help improve store layout, product mix, and shelf positioning. Recent innovations have enabled retailers to track customers' shopping patterns (e.g., footpath and time spent in different parts of a store), drawing real-time location data from smartphone applications (e.g., Shopkick), shopping cart transponders, or passively monitoring the location of mobile phones within a retail environment. Some retailers use sophisticated image-analysis software connected to their video-surveillance cameras to track in-store traffic patterns and consumer behavior.

4. **Customer micro-segmentation.** The next marketing-related big data lever is customer micro-segmentation. Although this is a familiar idea in retail, big data has enabled tremendous innovation in recent years. The amount of data available for segmentation has exploded, and the increasing sophistication in analytic tools has enabled the division into ever more granular micro-segments—to the point at which some retailers can claim to be engaged in personalization, rather than simply segmentation. In addition to using traditional market-research data and data on historical purchases, retailers can now track and leverage data on the behavior of individual customers—including clickstream data from the Web. Retailers can now update this increasingly granular data in near real time to adjust to customer changes. Neiman Marcus, a high-end retailer, has developed both behavioral segmentation and a multi-tier membership reward program, and this combination has led to substantially more purchases of higher margin products from its most affluent, higher-margin customers.

5. **Sentiment analysis.** Sentiment analysis leverages the voluminous streams of data generated by consumers in the various forms of social media to help inform a variety of business decisions. For example, retailers can use sentiment analysis to gauge the real-time response to marketing campaigns and adjust course accordingly. The evolving field of social media data analysis plays a key role because consumers are relying increasingly on peer sentiment and recommendations to make purchasing decisions. A variety of tools has emerged for the real-time monitoring and response to Web-based consumer behavior and choices.

6. **Enhancing the multichannel consumer experience.** Enhancing the multichannel experience for consumers can be a powerful driver of sales, customer satisfaction, and loyalty. Retailers can use big data to integrate promotions and pricing for shoppers seamlessly, whether those consumers are online, in-store, or perusing a catalog. Williams-Sonoma, for example, has integrated customer databases with information on some 60 million households, tracking such things as their income, housing values, and number of children. Targeted e-mails based on this information obtain ten to 18 times the response rate of e-mails that are not targeted, and the company is able to create different versions of its catalogs attuned to the behavior and preferences of different groups of customers.

---

63 ABI research, *Consumer Technology Barometer: Mobile*, 2010.

Merchandising

1. **Assortment optimization.** Deciding which products to carry in which stores based on local demographics, buyer perception, and other big data—so-called assortment optimization—can increase sales materially. One leading drug retailer, for example, used consumer research, market and competitive analysis, and detailed economic modeling to identify the causes of its flat and declining growth at the category level. It reduced its overall stock-keeping unit (SKU) count by 17 percent, shifted private-label brands from 10 percent of the product mix to 14 percent, and achieved a 3 percent earnings boost as well as a 2 percent increase in sales.

2. **Price optimization.** Retailers today can take advantage of the increasing granularity of data on pricing and sales and use higher levels of analytical horsepower to take pricing optimization to a new level. A variety of data sources can be used to assess and inform pricing decisions in near real time. Complex demand-elasticity models examine historical sales data to derive insights into pricing at the SKU level, including markdown pricing and scheduling. Retailers can use the resulting data to analyze promotion events and evaluate sources of sales lift and any underlying costs that these might entail. One food retailer examines pricing elasticity among its customers for different categories. Rural food consumers, for instance, see butter and rice as a higher buying priority and therefore these products are perhaps less price elastic than they would be for urban shoppers. Urban consumers, meanwhile, tend to rank cereals and candy higher among their priorities.

3. **Placement and design optimization.** Brick-and-mortar retailers can also gain substantially by optimizing the placement of goods and visual designs (e.g., end caps, shelves) by mining sales data at the SKU level—in essence, a more local version of the kinds of optimization that take advantage of foot-traffic data. Online retailers can adjust Web site placements based on data on page interaction such as scrolling, clicks, and mouse-overs. For instance, eBay has conducted thousands of experiments with different aspects of its Web site to determine optimal layout and other features from navigation to the size of its photos.

Operations

1. **Performance transparency.** Retailers can now run daily analyses of performance that they can aggregate and report by store sales, SKU sales, and sales per employee. Today, these systems are moving ever closer to real time. Retailers can look at cashiers for accuracy and transactions per hour and at the quality of customer service based on the percentage of customer issues solved with a single call, customer complaints, and satisfaction surveys. Although the industry already widely uses performance reporting at a basic level, the trend toward much higher frequency, immediacy, and granular reporting allows managers to make concrete adjustments in their operations in a much more timely manner, i.e., there is still headroom to gain value using this lever.

2. **Labor inputs optimization.** Another operational lever that can create value through reducing costs while maintaining service levels is around the optimization of labor inputs, automated time and attendance tracking, and improved labor scheduling. This lever can create more accurate predictions of staffing needs, especially during peak periods, so that overcapacity can be avoided. Because store labor represents approximately 30 percent of the average retailer's fixed costs, employing this lever is well worthwhile.

Supply chain

1. **Inventory management.** With the additional detail offered by advanced analytics mining multiple datasets, big data can continue to improve retailers' inventory management, Best-in-class inventory management provides full transparency at the SKU level, while bar code systems linked to automated replenishment processes reduce the incidents of running out of stock. Leading retailers are improving stock forecasting by combining multiple datasets such as sales histories, weather predictions, and seasonal sales cycles. Together, improved inventory management allows retailers to hold a lower level of stock because supplies are coupled much more tightly with demand signals, while reducing the number of sales lost because of merchandise stock-outs.

2. **Distribution and logistics optimization.** Leading retailers are also optimizing transportation by using GPS-enabled big data telematics (i.e., remote reporting of position, etc.) and route optimization to improve their fleet and distribution management. Transport analytics can improve productivity by optimizing fuel efficiency, preventive maintenance, driver behavior, and vehicle routing.

3. **Informing supplier negotiations.** In a big data world, leading retailers can analyze customer preferences and buying behavior to inform their negotiations with suppliers. They can use price and transaction data to focus negotiated concessions on key products, for instance. Using big data in this arena is a significant opportunity, given that the cost of goods sold makes up the largest portion of cost for a retailer. However, we should note that suppliers also recognize the importance of understanding customer preferences and are actively gaining access to, and analyzing, data on consumer behavior to uncover insights that strengthen their hand in negotiations with retailers.

New business models

The avalanche of data in the retail industry, coupled with other advances in business, is enabling the emergence of innovative business models. These models are the most intriguing and innovative—but also the most potentially threatening—to traditional retailers. Two new business models with the most traction today are price comparison services and Web based markets.

1. **Price comparison services.** It is common today for third parties to offer real time or near-real-time pricing and related price transparency on products across multiple retailers. Consumers can instantly compare the price of a specific product at multiple retail outlets. Where these comparisons are possible, prices tend to be lower. Studies show that consumers are saving an average of 10 percent when they can shop using such services. Retailers need to carefully think about how to respond to such price comparison services. Those that can compete on price will want to ensure that they are the most visible on such services. Retailers that cannot compete on price will need to determine how to differentiate themselves from competitors in a price-transparent world, whether it is in the quality of the shopping experience, differentiated products, or the provision of other value-added services.

2. **Web-based markets.** Web-based marketplaces, such as those provided by Amazon and eBay, provide searchable product listings from a large number of vendors. In addition to price transparency, they offer access to a vast number of niche retailers that otherwise do not have the marketing or sales horsepower to reach consumers. They also provide a tremendous amount of useful product information, including consumer-generated reviews that deliver further transparency to consumers.

Since we have drawn from global best practices, the findings of this case study can be applied to other countries and regions—with some qualifications. Developed economies will find the levers we identified and resulting analyses to be directly applicable. But the potential opportunities could be even larger in geographies that have not yet begun to use big data as a growth engine. In regions such as Europe where labor laws are relatively more rigid, the labor resource optimization levers may yield less dramatic results.

BIG DATA CAN DELIVER HIGHER MARGINS AND PRODUCTIVITY

We have estimated the potential impact of each of the 16 big data levers we have described, using a combination of our own case studies, academic and industry research, and interviews with experts; for more on our methodology, see the appendix. While we estimate the total potential value that big data can enable, we do not *predict* what value the sector will actually capture because this largely depends on actions taken by retailers to overcome a number of barriers, including obstacles related to technology, talent, and culture, as well as external factors such as whether consumers are receptive to having their behavior data mined and the ability of suppliers to leverage some of the same levers in negotiations.

Marketing levers can affect 10 to 30 percent of operating margin; merchandising levers can affect 10 to 40 percent; and supply chain levers can have a 5 to 35 percent impact (Exhibit 23). In contrast, price transparency levers will tend to cut prices and squeeze margins.

The total potential impact of individual big data levers varies significantly across retail subsectors (Exhibit 24). Some subsectors will have already pulled big data levers more than others, partly explaining this variation.

Exhibit 23

Different levers have varied impacts on the operating margins of firms

Impact on operating margin

%

-30
-20
-10
0
10
20
30
40
50
Marketing
Merchandising
Operations
Supply chain
Price transparency

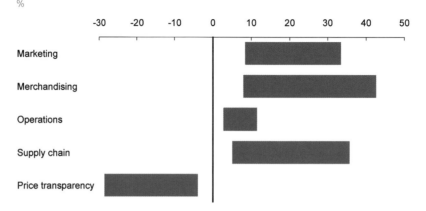

SOURCE: Expert interviews; publicly available data; McKinsey case studies; McKinsey Global Institute analysis

Exhibit 24

The big data value potential in retail varies in different subsectors

Highest relevance

Lowest relevance

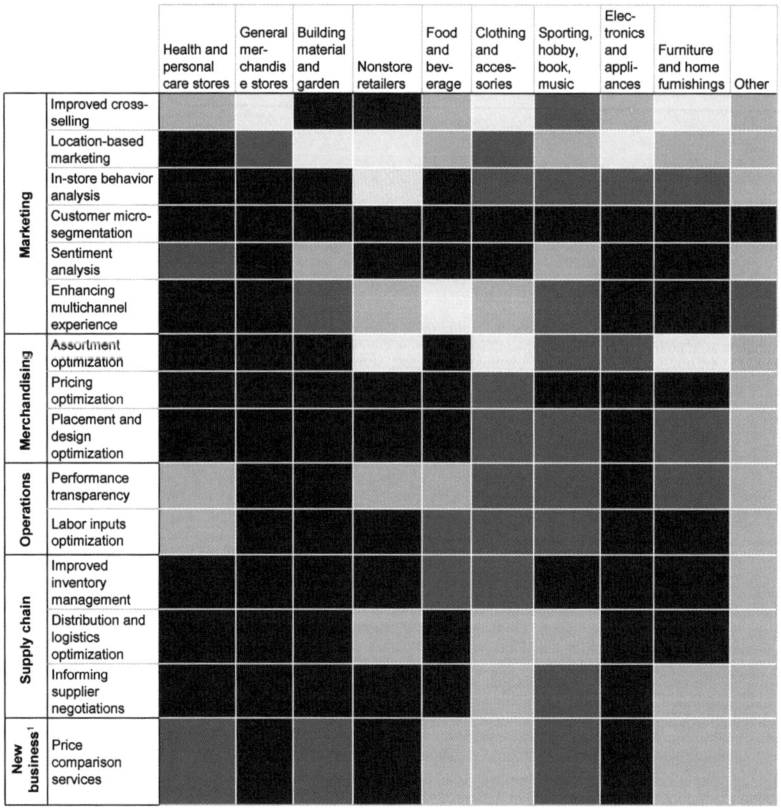

Health and personal care stores
General merchandise stores
Building material and garden
Nonstore retailers
Food and beverage
Clothing and accessories
Sporting, hobby, book, music
Electronics and appliances
Furniture and home furnishings
Other
Marketing
Improved cross-selling
Location-based marketing
In-store behavior analysis
Customer micro-segmentation
Sentiment analysis
Enhancing multichannel experience
Merchandising
Assortment optimization
Pricing optimization
Placement and design optimization
Operations
Performance transparency
Labor inputs optimization
Supply chain
Improved inventory management
Distribution and logistics optimization
Informing supplier negotiations
New business[1]
Price comparison services

1 Impact of Web-based markets is very difficult to quantify and this has not been included here.

SOURCE: McKinsey Global Institute analysis

While individual players can use big data levers to grow their top lines and operating margins, these gains will largely shift value within the industry rather than increasing its total size. Firms that are relatively better at deploying big data levers will experience significant gains at the expense of those that do not execute as well. The overall winners should be consumers, who will benefit from receiving goods better suited to their needs.

We also estimated potential productivity gains at the industry level, opting to take a conservative approach to such estimates by applying only the effects of levers in operations and supply chains that reduce costs (see the appendix for detail on our methodology). If we look solely at efficiency, we estimate that big data levers have the potential to create an annual 0.5 percent acceleration in productivity through 2020. To put that in context, academic research has estimated that IT investments in the entire US economy, including retail, through the high-growth 1990s added 1 to 2 percent to the compound annual growth rate of US productivity.[64]

This estimate does not take into account the fact that the use of big data will be a boon to consumers through the economic surplus that they will capture and is therefore conservative. For instance, even if retail consumers do not spend more money overall, many of the marketing and merchandising levers we have described will improve their shopping experience. Consumers will find better products to match their needs (e.g., consumers that choose to opt-in to marketing programs that use big data to better target offers) and spend less time looking for those products at the right price (e.g., because they can obtain information about the availability of inventory before visiting a store, or use price comparison services). This should increase the real value added of the retail sector, even if estimating the value of this consumer surplus is difficult.

We believe that the use of large datasets will continue to transform the face of retail. In recent decades, IT and data that was used to optimize supply chains helped create the category of big-box retailers that sell large volumes of a wide range of products at low prices. In recent years, online retailers such as Amazon, eBay, and Groupon are redefining what retail can mean. Instead of receiving information about goods and services from sales teams or advertisements, consumers find the information they need from their fellow shoppers and find what they want to buy via electronic marketplaces.

THE INDUSTRY AND POLICY MAKERS NEED TO OVERCOME BARRIERS TO TAP THE FULL OPPORTUNITY OF BIG DATA

If the retail industry is to realize the potential value from the use of big data, both the industry and government will have to deal with a number of important barriers. Policy makers will make choices about how to regulate the industry's use of information about consumers—policy choices that will have profound implications for many other industries that, in common with retail, will draw increasingly pronounced concerns about privacy and security in the era of big data. It is certainly the case that consumer attitudes toward the use of their personal information, especially personal location data and electronic data generated by their use of the Internet, are changing rapidly. But many people remain uninformed about how, where, and to what extent this information is used in targeted advertising and other marketing strategies.

---

64 Stephen Oliner and Daniel Sichel, "Information technology and productivity: Where we are now and where we are going?", Federal Reserve Bank of Atlanta *Economic Review*, 2002.

Across the globe, we observe the emergence of different concepts of electronic privacy. Germany, for instance, has limited the use of the Street View function of Google maps. Depending on the jurisdiction and purpose, there are different definitions of personally identifiable information (PII)—what counts legally as information that identifies a person for a variety of purposes. Some definitions are more general than others, and large players would benefit from having a single country or industry standard.

For their part, retail executives must manage and overcome multiple barriers to realize the full potential of big data. The first is the mind-set of employees and firms; many people still view IT as a back-office function and therefore as a large cost center rather than as an engine for business growth. In contrast, leading companies in their use of big data understand that their IT initiatives will be a crucial source of competitive advantage. These companies must make sure that business and IT leaders collaborate closely so that the use of big data underpins improvements in efficiency improvement and opportunities for creating value. Companies should also actively seek out and implement big-data-based innovations that will give them long-term competitive advantages.

Another common obstacle for big data leaders is their legacy IT systems. Many of these systems were installed decades ago, well before today's big data opportunities were considered or even possible. These legacy systems usually include multiple silos of information generated in incompatible standards and formats so that they cannot be readily integrated, accessed, and analyzed. Attempts to upgrade and integrate these systems can be so difficult and plagued with the potential for introducing new system bugs that one retail expert complained that such an effort was "much worse than starting from scratch."

Even deploying new IT-enabled systems can present tremendous challenges. The gap between the predicted scale of adoption of RFID systems and their actual deployment tells a cautionary tale. RFID held the promise of providing a source of supply chain data that could be exploited using big data techniques. In the early days, RFID reader reliability was far worse than originally expected, necessitating manual inputs to correct for reader errors. This destroyed the productivity gains expected from deploying this technology. Adoption slowed, RFID tags were in lower demand, and per-tag costs did not decline as quickly as anticipated, as economies of scale were muted. Higher tag prices hurt the business case for further RFID deployment, reinforcing a negative cycle in which the application of big data levers based on this technology has been delayed.

Potentially as daunting for retail executives is the task of finding the talent that can execute big data levers. Globally, executives complain about the scarcity of high-quality candidates for these jobs, and many retailers do not have sufficient talent in-house. Moreover, existing analytical and technical talent tends to be managed inefficiently, isolated in particular departments, or scattered in different business units. People with the requisite skills are rarely directly involved in strategic decision making and have little impact beyond answering highly specific questions. Retailers with the foresight and intelligence to hire big data talent in sufficient numbers and then involve these hires in strategic decisions and planning will take the fullest advantage of value-creation opportunities at the expense of their less nimble competitors.

☐ ☐ ☐

In an environment in which retailers face significant pressures from slow GDP growth in conjunction with pricing pressures from suppliers upstream and consumers downstream, retailers need to compete fiercely to ensure their survival and relevance. While information technology and data have already delivered waves of impact, our research finds that there is significant headroom arising out of innovation that retailers can tap. Retailers that develop and exercise their big data muscles will boost their chances of outcompeting and winning at the expense of those who do not grasp this opportunity in the years ahead.

3d. Manufacturing (global)

The manufacturing sector was an early and intensive user of data to drive quality and efficiency, adopting information technology and automation to design, build, and distribute products since the dawn of the computer era. In the 1990s, manufacturing companies racked up impressive annual productivity gains because of both operational improvements that increased the efficiency of their manufacturing processes and improvements in the quality of products they manufactured. For example, advanced manufactured products such as computers became much more powerful. Manufacturers also optimized their global footprints by placing sites in, or outsourcing production to, low-cost regions. But despite such advances, manufacturing, arguably more than most other sectors, faces the challenge of generating significant productivity improvement in industries that have already become relatively efficient. We believe that big data can underpin another substantial wave of gains.[65]

These gains will come from improved efficiency in design and production, further improvements in product quality, and better meeting customer needs through more precisely targeted products and effective promotion and distribution. For example, big data can help manufacturers reduce product development time by 20 to 50 percent and eliminate defects prior to production through simulation and testing. Using real-time data, companies can also manage demand planning across extended enterprises and global supply chains, while reducing defects and rework within production plants. Overall, big data provides a means to achieve dramatic improvements in the management of the complex, global, extended value chains that are becoming prevalent in manufacturing and to meet customers' needs in innovative and more precise ways, such as through collaborative product development based on customer data.

We base these conclusions on an examination of multiple manufacturing subsectors encompassing both discrete and process manufacturing, from basic manufacturing subsectors such as consumer goods and food, to advanced manufacturing subsectors such as automotive and aerospace. We drew upon global best practice examples of the use of big data to identify seven levers of value creation, describe the range of potential impact, and the barriers that have to be overcome to capture that value.[66]

MANUFACTURING HAS HISTORICALLY BEEN A PRODUCTIVITY LEADER, AND BIG DATA CAN HELP EXTEND GAINS

The manufacturing sector has been the backbone of many developed economies and remains an important driver of GDP and employment there. However, with the rise of production capacity and capability in China and other low-cost nations, manufacturing has become an increasingly global activity, featuring extended supply chains made possible by advances in information and communications technology. While globalization is not a recent phenomenon, the explosion in information and communication technology, along with reduced international freight costs and lower entry barriers to markets worldwide, has hugely accelerated the industrial

---

65 Manufacturing is a sector with multiple issues that advanced economies need to address, many of which do not involve big data. In this research, we focus on the role that big data can play.

66 Our analysis focuses primarily on the core production processes of a manufacturer—i.e., R&D, supply chain, and manufacturing processes—and less on adjacent processes such as marketing and sales.

development path and created increasingly complex webs of value chains spanning the world.[67]

Increasingly global and fragmented manufacturing value chains create new challenges that manufacturers must overcome to sustain productivity growth. In many cases, technological change and globalization have allowed countries to specialize in specific stages of the production process. As a result, manufacturers have assembled global production and supply chain networks to achieve cost advantages. For example, a typical global consumer electronics manufacturer has production facilities on almost every continent, weighing logistics costs against manufacturing costs to optimize the footprint of their facilities. Advanced manufacturers also often have a large number of suppliers, specialized in producing specific types of components where they have sustainable advantages both in cost and quality. It is typical for a large automobile original equipment manufacturer (OEM) assembly plant to be supplied by up to 4,000 outside vendors.

To continue achieving high levels of productivity growth, manufacturers will need to leverage large datasets to drive efficiency across the extended enterprise and to design and market higher-quality products. The "raw material" is readily available; manufacturers already have a significant amount of digital data with which to work. Manufacturing stores more data than any other sector—close to 2 exabytes of new data stored in 2010. This sector generates data from a multitude of sources, from instrumented production machinery (process control), to supply chain management systems, to systems that monitor the performance of products that have already been sold (e.g., during a single cross-country flight, a Boeing 737 generates 240 terabytes of data).

And the amount of data generated will continue to grow exponentially. The number of RFID tags sold globally is projected to rise from 12 million in 2011 to 209 billion in 2021. IT systems installed along the value chain to monitor the extended enterprise are creating additional stores of increasingly complex data, which currently tends to reside only in the IT system where it is generated. Manufacturers will also begin to combine data from different systems including, for example, computer-aided design, computer-aided engineering, computer-aided manufacturing, collaborative product development management, and digital manufacturing, and across organizational boundaries in, for instance, end-to-end supply chain data.

MANUFACTURERS CAN USE BIG DATA ACROSS THE VALUE CHAIN

Big data has the potential to enable seven performance improvement levers for manufacturers, affecting the entire value chain (Exhibit 25). In this section, we will discuss each of these in turn.

Research and development and product design

The use of big data offers further opportunities to accelerate product development, help designers home in on the most important and valuable features based on concrete customer inputs as well as designs that minimize production costs, and harness consumer insights to reduce development costs through approaches including open innovation.

---

67 While the transition to a post-industrial economy took about 200 years in the United Kingdom and about 130 years in Germany, South Korea took about 60 years. See Eberhard Abele, Tobias Meyer, Ulrich Näher, Gernot Strube, and Richard Sykes, eds., *Global production: A handbook for strategy and implementation* (Berlin: Springer, 2008).

Exhibit 25

We have identified the following big data levers across the manufacturing value chain

	R&D and design	Supply-chain mgmt	Production	Marketing and sales	After-sales service
1 Build consistent **interoperable, cross-functional R&D and product design databases** along supply chain to enable concurrent engineering, rapid experimentation and simulation, and co-creation	✓				
2 **Aggregate customer data and make them widely available** to improve service level, capture cross- and up-selling opportunities, and enable **design-to-value**	✓				
3 Source and share data through **virtual collaboration sites** (**idea marketplaces** to enable crowd sourcing)	✓				
4 Implement advanced **demand forecasting and supply planning** across suppliers and using external variables		✓			
5 Implement **lean manufacturing and model production virtually (digital factory)** to create process transparency, develop dashboards, and visualize bottlenecks			✓		
6 Implement **sensor data-driven operations analytics** to improve throughput and enable mass customization			✓		
7 Collect **after-sales data from sensors** and feed back in real time to trigger after-sales services and detect manufacturing or design flaws					✓

SOURCE: McKinsey Global Institute analysis

1. **Product lifecycle management.** Over decades, manufacturing companies have implemented IT systems to manage the product lifecycle including computer aided-design, engineering, manufacturing, and product development management tools, and digital manufacturing. However, the large datasets generated by these systems have tended to remain trapped within their respective systems. Manufacturers could capture a significant big data opportunity to create more value by instituting product lifecycle management (PLM) platforms that can integrate datasets from multiple systems to enable effective and consistent collaboration. For example, PLM could provide a platform for "co-creation," e.g., bringing together internal and external inputs to create new products. This is particularly useful in fields such as aerospace where a new product might be assembled with hundreds of thousands of components supplied by hundreds of suppliers from around the world. In this context, having the OEM co-create designs with suppliers can be extraordinarily valuable. PLM platforms can also significantly enable experimentation at the design stage. Designers and manufacturing engineers can share data and quickly and cheaply create simulations to test different designs, the choice of parts and suppliers, and the associated manufacturing costs. This is especially useful because decisions made in the design stage typically drive 80 percent of manufacturing costs.

   Leading players in advanced industries are already embracing the collaborative use of data and controlled experimentation. Toyota, Fiat, and Nissan have all cut new-model development time by 30 to 50 percent; Toyota claims to have eliminated 80 percent of defects prior to building the first physical prototype.[68] However, while the payoff for this opportunity is large, manufacturers will likely need to invest significantly upgrade their systems, which in many cases are decades old. In addition to the technical work of integrating datasets from

---

68 Note that in addition to reducing development time, manufacturers, as a result of using integrated PLM, are able to improve quality and reduce resources in order to develop more derivatives or product extensions.

different IT systems, manufacturers will need to ensure that staff members from different functions (R&D, production) and organizations (OEMs, suppliers) use these tools to collaborate. Today, a lack of collaboration across silos is closer to the norm.

2. **Design to value.** While obtaining customer input through market research has traditionally been a part of the product design process, many manufacturers have yet to systematically extract crucial insights from the increasing volume of customer data to refine existing designs and help develop specifications for new models and variants. Best-in-class manufacturers conduct conjoint analyses to determine how much customers are willing to pay for certain features and to understand which features are most important for success in the market.[69] These companies supplement such efforts with additional quantitative customer insights mined from sources such as point-of-sales data and customer feedback. New sources of data that manufacturers are starting to mine include customer comments in social media and sensor data that describe actual product usage.

However, gaining access to comprehensive data about customers in order to achieve holistic insights can be a significant barrier for manufacturers; distributors, retailers, and other players can be unwilling to share such data, considering them to be a competitive asset. Nevertheless, the size of the prize for successfully designing to value can be substantial, especially in subsectors with high product differentiation and changing customer preferences. For example, one manufacturer of telecom equipment used customer insights data to improve gross margin by 30 percent in 24 months, eliminating unnecessary costly features and adding those that had higher value to the customer and for which the customer was willing to pay a higher price.

3. **Open innovation.** To drive innovation and develop products that address emerging customer needs, manufacturers are relying increasingly on outside inputs through innovative channels. With the advent of Web 2.0, some manufacturers are inviting external stakeholders to submit ideas for innovations or even collaborate on product development via Web-based platforms. Consumer goods companies such as Kraft and Procter and Gamble invite ideas from their consumers as well as collaborate with external experts, including academics and industry researchers, to develop new products. In the early 2000s, P&G faced a problem of rising R&D costs but a declining payoff. In response, the company created the Connect and Develop open innovation program, one element of which was leveraging InnoCentive, a Web-based platform that invites experts to solve technical challenges that P&G is facing. Today, half of new products have elements that originated outside the company, up from 15 percent in 2000. R&D productivity at P&G is up 60 percent, and R&D as a share of revenue has fallen from 4.8 to 3.4 percent. But as successful as these open innovation initiatives can be, one key problem is how to extract, in an efficient way, the truly valuable ideas from the potentially large number of inputs these programs can generate. This is a task that big data techniques such as automated algorithms can help to solve.

Open innovation through big data has been extended to advanced industries as well. BMW, for example, has created an "idea management system" to help evaluate ideas submitted through its "virtual innovation agency." This has cut the

---

69 Conjoint analysis is a statistical technique that involves providing a controlled set of potential products and services to elicit end users' preferences through which an implicit valuation of individual elements that make up the product or service can be determined.

time taken to identify high-potential ideas by 50 percent and has also reduced the time it takes to make a decision about how feasible an idea is. The result has been that the company has incorporated two or three major ideas from its open innovation effort into its models every year. An additional benefit of these open innovation techniques is that they create more brand engagement from participants in these efforts, as well as a positive "halo" effect as these initiatives become more widely recognized.

Supply chain

Manufacturers, especially those producing fast-moving consumer goods, have significant additional opportunities to improve demand forecasting and supply chain planning. The volatility of demand has been a critical issue for manufacturers. Their retailing customers have pushed hard for increased flexibility and responsiveness from suppliers, given the diverging and ever-changing preferences of consumers. Other trends, such as the increasing use of promotions and tactical pricing, have only magnified volatility issues facing suppliers.

Manufacturers can improve their demand forecasting and supply planning by the improved use of their own data. But as we've seen in other domains, far more value can be unlocked when companies are able to integrate data from other sources including data from retailers, such as promotion data (e.g., items, prices, sales), launch data (e.g., specific items to be listed/delisted, ramp-up/ramp-down plans), and inventory data (e.g., stock levels per warehouse, sales per store). By taking into account data from across the value chain (potentially through collaborative supply chain management and planning), manufacturers can smooth spiky order patterns. The benefits of doing so will ripple through the value chain, helping manufacturers to use cash more effectively and to deliver a higher level of service. Best-in-class manufacturers are also accelerating the frequency of planning cycles to synchronize them with production cycles. Indeed, some manufacturers are using near-real-time data to adjust production. Others are collaborating with retailers to shape demand at the store level with time-based discounts.

Production

Big data are driving additional efficiency in the production process with the application of simulation techniques to the already large volume of data that production generates. The increasing deployment of the "Internet of Things" is also allowing manufacturers to use real-time data from sensors to track parts, monitor machinery, and guide actual operations.[70]

1. **Digital factory.** Taking inputs from product development and historical production data (e.g., order data, machine performance), manufacturers can apply advanced computational methods to create a digital model of the entire manufacturing process. Such a "digital factory"—including all machinery, labor, and fixtures—can be used to design and simulate the most efficient production system, from layout to sequencing of steps, for a specific product. Leading automobile manufacturers have used this technique to optimize the production layout of new plants, particularly when there are myriad constraints such as space and utility distribution. A steel manufacturer used simulation to model its entire portfolio of factories and quickly test improvement levers; this led to an

---

70 "Internet of Things" refers to sensors and actuators within networks of physical objects. For more information, see Michael Chui, Markus Löffler, and Roger Roberts, "The Internet of Things," *McKinsey Quarterly*, March 2010.

improvement in delivery reliability of 20 to 30 percentage points. Case studies in automotive, aerospace and defense, and semiconductors show that these types of advanced simulations can reduce the number of production-drawing changes as well as the cost of tool design and construction.[71] Plants designed with these techniques also have realized substantial reductions in assembly hours, cost savings, and even improved delivery reliability.

2. **Sensor-driven operations.** The proliferation of Internet of Things applications allows manufacturers to optimize operations by embedding real-time, highly granular data from networked sensors in the supply chain and production processes. These data allows ubiquitous process control and optimization to reduce waste and maximize yield or throughput. They even allow for innovations in manufacturing that have not been possible thus far, including nano manufacturing.[72]

Some of the best examples of using big data from sensor networks come from process manufacturing such as oil refining. For decades, the oil industry has used huge amounts of real-time data to develop ever more hard-to-reach deposits. Now, the industry has extended its use of big data to the production side to the automated, remotely monitored oil field. The benefit of this approach is that it cuts operations and maintenance costs that can account for 60 percent of wasted expenses. In the digital oil field, a single system captures data from well-head flow monitors, seismic sensors, and satellite telemetry systems. The data are transmitted to very large data farms and then relayed to a real-time operations center that monitors and adjusts parameters to optimize production and minimize downtime. Experience suggests that the digital oil field can cut operational costs by 10 to 25 percent even while potentially boosting production by 5 percent or more.

Marketing and sales/after-sales support

As we have described, manufacturing companies are using data from customer interactions not only to improve marketing and sales but also to inform product development decisions. Increasingly, it is economically feasible to embed sensors in products that can "phone home," generating data about actual product usage and performance. Manufacturers can now obtain real-time input on emerging defects and adjust the production process immediately. R&D operations can share these data for redesign and new product development. Many construction equipment manufacturers already embed sensors in their products, and this can provide granular real-time data about utilization and usage patterns, enabling these manufacturers to improve demand forecasts as well as their future product development.

There are also many opportunities to leverage large datasets in the marketing, sales, and after-sales service activities. As we can observe in many sectors, opportunities range from the segmentation of customers to applying analytics in order to improve the effectiveness of sales forces. An increasingly important application for manufacturers is using sensor data from products once they are in use to improve service offerings. For example, analyzing the data reported by sensors embedded in complex products enables manufacturers of aircraft, elevators, and data-center servers to create proactive smart preventive maintenance service packages. A repair

---

71 See for example, U. Bracht and T. Masurat, "The Digital Factory between vision and reality," *Computers in Industry* 56(4), May 2005.

72 An example is nano-scale printing in semiconductors.

82

technician can be dispatched before the customer even realizes that a component is likely to fail. Other manufacturers have been able to transform the commercial relationship with customers from one in which they sell a product to one in which they sell a service. An example is jet engine manufacturers selling "power-by-the-hour."

BIG DATA IN AGGREGATE UNDERPINS SUBSTANTIAL PRODUCTIVITY POTENTIAL AND INNOVATION

For manufacturers, opportunities enabled by big data can drive productivity gains both through improving efficiency and the quality of products (Exhibit 26).[73] Efficiency gains arise across the value chain, from reducing unnecessary iterations in product development cycles to optimizing the assembly process. The real output value of products is increased by improving their quality and making products that better match customers' needs.

Exhibit 26

Big data levers can deliver value along the manufacturing value chain in terms of cost, revenue, and working capital

| | Lever examples | Impact | | | Subsector applicability |
		Cost	Revenue	Working capital	
R&D and design	▪ Concurrent engineering/PLM[1] ▪ Design-to-value ▪ Crowd sourcing	+20–50% PD[2] costs +30% gross margin -25% PD[2] costs	-20-50% time to market		High – Low complexity High – Low complexity B2C – B2B
Supply chain management	▪ Demand forecasting/ shaping and supply planning	+2–3% profit margin		-3–7% onetime	FMCG[3] – Capital goods
Production	▪ Sensor data-driven operations analytics ▪ "Digital Factory" for lean manufacturing	-10–25% operating costs -10–50% assembly costs	Up to +7% revenue +2% revenue		Capital intense – CPG[3] Capital intense – CPG[3]
After-sales services	▪ Product sensor data analysis for after-sales service	-10–40% maintenance costs	+10% annual production		Capital intense – CPG[3]

1 Product lifecycle management.
2 Product development.
3 Fast-moving consumer goods and consumer packaged goods
SOURCE: Expert interviews; press and literature search; McKinsey Global Institute analysis

Beyond pushing productivity, big data enables innovative services and even new business models in manufacturing. Sensor data have made possible innovative after-sales services. For example, BMW's ConnectedDrive offers drivers directions based on real-time traffic information, automatically calling for help when sensors indicate trouble, alerts drivers of maintenance needs based on the actual condition of the car, and feeds operation data directly to service centers. The ability to track the use of products at a micro-level has also made possible monetization models that are based not on the purchase of a product but on services priced by their usage, as we have described. The ability to exchange data across the extended enterprise has also enabled production to be unbundled radically into highly distributed networks. For example, Li and Fung, a supplier to apparel retailers, orchestrates a network of more than 7,500 suppliers, each of which focuses on delivering a very specific part of the supply chain.

---

73 Gains will likely show up in both labor productivity and resource productivity.

Some of the most powerful impacts of big data apply across entire manufacturing ecosystems. As we have documented, big data plays a pivotal role in ensuring that these ecosystem webs function well and continue to evolve. Indeed, new data intermediaries or data businesses could begin to emerge. They could, for example, capitalize on the economic value of data that describes the flow of goods around the world.

MANUFACTURERS MUST TACKLE ORGANIZATIONAL, CULTURAL, AND TALENT CHALLENGES TO MAXIMIZE THE BENEFITS OF BIG DATA

Much of the value that big data can create in manufacturing requires the access and varied use of data from multiple sources across an extended enterprise. So to fulfill the potential for value creation in this sector will require manufacturing companies to invest in IT as well as to make organizational changes. The additional IT investment necessary may not be insignificant. Some of the big data levers that we have discussed, including updating a PLM platform that can link across various IT systems, will be costly. Nevertheless, the long-term payoff should outweigh the cost. Other investments will be required to develop interfaces and protocols to share data effectively across the extended enterprise. The standardization of interfaces will be critical and may require industry-wide partnerships to achieve. Strongly departmentalized companies, with multiple IT systems and overlapping and/or redundant data in different operations and divisions, are clearly at a disadvantage. To obtain the benefits of design-to-value, for instance, a company needs to have a free interchange of data among marketing and sales, R&D, and production. So, in many organizations, achieving success will require strong leadership and a cultural shift to establish the mind-sets and behaviors to breech today's silos. Many organizations will need to undertake organizational change programs to enforce the necessary shift—groups that have never shared their data will not start to do so simply because the IT systems are in place.

Many of the levers also require access to data from different players in the value chain. To optimize production planning, data from various tiers of suppliers will be necessary. Demand planning will require customer data from retailers. To access such pools of data, manufacturers will need to be thoughtful about establishing the right value propositions and incentives. Many retailers, for instance, guard customer data as proprietary, but there have been instances of successful data sharing. A notable example is the vendor-managed inventory model between some large retailers and consumer packaged goods companies, pioneered on a significant scale by Wal-Mart, as we discussed in our retail case study.

Manufacturing companies will also need to build the capabilities needed to manage big data. Despite the fact that the sector has been dealing with large datasets for two decades, the rising volume of data from new sources along the supply chain and from end markets requires a new level of storage and computing power and deep analytical expertise if manufacturers are to harvest relevant information and insights. There is a shortage of talent with the right experience for managing this level of complexity. Manufacturers will need not only to recruit new talent but also to remove organizational obstacles that today prevent such individuals from making maximum contributions. For example, we know of oil refineries that still rely on a manager with spreadsheets to plan equipment maintenance and upgrades—work that can be accomplished more effectively with algorithms using data collected directly from machinery.

Finally, where big data applications touch consumers and other end users, there are privacy issues. One of the most promising ideas is using product sensor data to create finely targeted after-sales services or cross-selling. But wielding this lever will be possible only if consumers don't object to suppliers monitoring how they use their products. Manufacturers must therefore address privacy concerns proactively, in collaboration with policy makers, and communicate with end users about choices and data transparency.

☐ ☐ ☐

Manufacturers have tremendous potential to generate value from the use of large datasets, integrating data across the extended enterprise and applying advanced analytical techniques to raise their productivity both by increasing efficiency and improving the quality of their products. In emerging markets, manufacturers can begin to build competitive advantage that goes beyond their (thus far) relatively low labor costs. In developed markets, manufacturers can use big data to reduce costs and deliver greater innovation in products and services.

3e. Personal location data (global)

We are witnessing an explosion in the amount of information available about where people are in the world. Technologies such as GPS allow us to quickly locate a device as small as a mobile phone within a few dozen meters, and we are seeing personal location data being used to create a wave of new businesses and innovative business models that are touching the lives of people around the globe. This revolution will continue over the next decade and beyond with opportunities unfolding that we cannot even imagine. The quality, accessibility, and volume of personal location data will improve and expand, reaching into many business sectors and creating transformational financial opportunities well beyond those that we are witnessing today.

Unlike the other domains that we have examined, new pools of personal location data are not confined to a single sector but rather cut across many industries, including telecom, retail, and media. This domain offers the potential for huge new value creation over the next ten years that we estimate at more than $100 billion in revenue to service providers and as much as $700 billion in value to consumer and business end users. Capturing this value will require the right enablers, including sufficient investment in technology, infrastructure, and personnel as well as appropriate government action.

PERSONAL LOCATION DATA VOLUMES HAVE INCREASED RAPIDLY WITH GROWTH IN THE ADOPTION OF MOBILE PHONES

In this analysis, we examined personal location data that pinpoint accurately—within a few city blocks—where a person (or a device) is in real time, usually expressed in digital code that maps an individual's location on a grid stretched across the earth's surface (see Box 10, "How did we define the scope of personal location data?"). An early source of personal location data was individuals' credit and debit card payments, linked to personal identification data from cards swiped at point-of-sale (POS) terminals typically in fixed locations. A similar connection was possible using transactions made at automated teller machines. Globally in 2008, there were 90 billion to 100 billion such transactions off line linkable to POS devices. Law enforcement investigations regularly use such data to establish physical location.

As the number of people using mobile phones has increased, the use of cell-tower signals to triangulate the location of such devices has become increasingly common. This technology has the potential to identify the location of the owners of almost 5 billion globally. The penetration of smartphones is increasing, too. In 2010, about 600 million devices were already in use, and their number is projected to grow at about 20 percent per year. Smartphones are enabled with GPS, a technology that triangulates location within about 15 meters using a constellation of orbiting satellites. Many smartphones also have Wi-Fi networking capability, an additional source of data to determine location. Services such as Skyhook have mapped the physical location of various Wi-Fi networks that broadcast their identity (service set identifier, or SSID) and therefore allow a mobile device to correlate the Wi-Fi networks it detects with a physical location. These smartphone technologies are making personal location data more accurate and far more readily available, particularly to developers of mobile device applications.

In addition, new technologies are being developed that determine personal location within buildings where GPS signals are notoriously weak. Shopkick is a mobile phone application that allows merchants to track their customers from the moment they walk into a store by picking up inaudible sounds emitted by in-store devices on the mobile phone's microphone. Another example of such innovation is UK-based company Path Intelligence, which can track foot traffic within malls or amusement parks by passively monitoring identification signals sent by individual mobile phones.

Box 10. How did we define the scope of personal location data?

For the purposes of this analysis, we include technologies that locate an individual within a few intersections (i.e., within a couple of city blocks in an urban setting and perhaps beyond those parameters in less densely populated areas) and increasingly with even finer precision. Today, there are three primary sources of these data: GPS chips in mobile devices such as phones and personal navigation systems; cell-tower triangulation data on mobile devices; and in-person card payment data linked to a POS terminal. We do not include data derived from Internet Protocol addresses because the margin of error varies widely according to whether the device to which the IP address is attached is mobile, and to the density and topology of the underlying IP network. In addition, our analysis leaves out data about the relative distances between locations without absolute coordinates, such as data derived from watches that track running distances and various motion sensors.

We have also excluded location data about non-human objects such as packages being tracked as inventory, or shipping containers that have been tagged with GPS sensors. Tracking the location of objects can enable a tremendous amount of economic value. For example, the global location of high-value and/or perishable goods while in shipment, e.g., pharmaceuticals or high-tech components, is data of great value to both the suppliers and customers of these products. Some logistics companies are already offering the capability to provide these data to their customers, combining location with other data from sensors on-board the packages carrying these goods, e.g., the temperature or physical shocks they have endured while in transit. Some of the benefits of tracking the location of objects have already been evident in our research on retail and manufacturing. For this case study, we studied applications of location data about individuals in order to focus on a set of new and emerging applications, and to constrain our research to a manageable scope.

A combination of navigation devices, cell-tower tracking, and smartphones accounts for the majority of personal location data today. Navigation devices are a major source of data volume because they update their locations so frequently. Cell towers generate a high volume of personal location data simply because there are so many cell phone users worldwide. And smartphones are a huge and fast-growing source of these data because the majority of users use applications that require their locations to be tracked.

Our research estimates that the global pool of generated personal location data was at least 1 petabyte in 2009 and that this pool is growing by about 20 percent a year (Exhibit 27).[74] (Note that we do not include the potential amount of data from cell-tower triangulation.)[75] Explosive growth in the use of GPS-enabled smartphones is

---

74 A petabyte is the equivalent of about 20 million four-drawer filing cabinets full of text.

75 We did not include location data inferred from cell-tower triangulation because the locations are relatively imprecise. Including those data would have increased our estimate of the size of personal location data 400-fold, given that the nearest cell-tower signals are determined every seven seconds.

the major driver of this expansion.[76] Compared with other sectors, such as health care, that measure the size of total data in exabytes (1 exabyte is 1,000 times a PB), the total size of pure personal location data is relatively small because the amount of data required to capture a single location fix is only a few bytes while each image or video is sized in megabytes. However, the relatively small amount of data generated by the personal location domain suggests that this type of data potentially offer a much higher value per byte generated, as we will discuss.

Exhibit 27

Overall personal location data total more than 1 petabyte per year globally

Personal location data generated globally, 2009

Terabytes

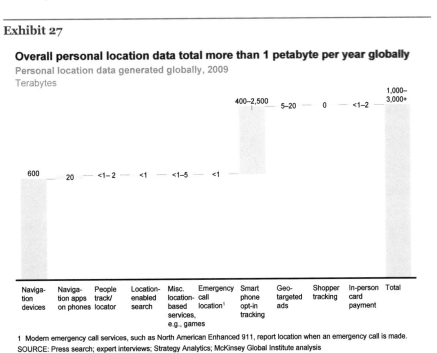

1 Modern emergency call services, such as North American Enhanced 911, report location when an emergency call is made.
SOURCE: Press search; expert interviews; Strategy Analytics; McKinsey Global Institute analysis

Asia is the leading region for the generation of personal location data simply because so many mobile phones are in use there. For instance, China has more mobile phones in use than in any other country at an estimated 800 million devices in 2010. India ranks second in this regard with more than 650 million mobile phones in use, dwarfing the North America in third place with its 300 million cell phones in 2010. Growth in the use of mobile telephony is set to grow rapidly in developing markets, particularly the use of advanced devices, is set to grow rapidly in developing markets.[77] In China, for instance, we expect the number of basic phones to shrink at a rate of 13 percent per year between 2010 and 2015, but the use of devices with smart features to increase by an estimated 5 percent annually during this period, and that of advanced phones by a stunning 33 percent. We anticipate broadly similar trends to unfold in India (Exhibit 28).

76 Location data generated by smartphones and their applications are growing at double the average rate of growth for all location data (which also includes for example navigation devices) because of the rapid growth of smartphone adoption.

77 Yankee Group divides mobile phones into three categories: basic phones, smart features, and advanced operating system (OS). Advanced operating system (OS) maps most closely to the meaning of smartphones used in the media today. See *Global mobile forecast*, Yankee Group, December 2010.

Exhibit 28

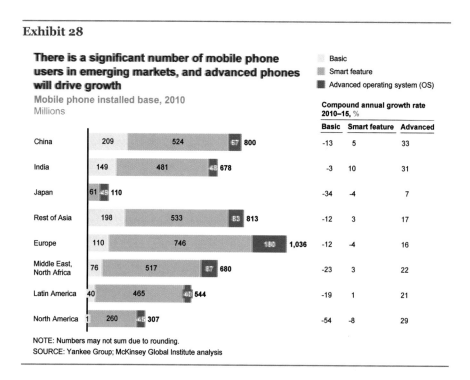

There is a significant number of mobile phone users in emerging markets, and advanced phones will drive growth

Mobile phone installed base, 2010
Millions

		Compound annual growth rate 2010–15, %		
		Basic	Smart feature	Advanced
China	209 / 524 / 67 = 800	-13	5	33
India	149 / 481 / 48 = 678	-3	10	31
Japan	61 / 49 = 110	-34	-4	7
Rest of Asia	198 / 533 / 83 = 813	-12	3	17
Europe	110 / 746 / 180 = 1,036	-12	-4	16
Middle East, North Africa	76 / 517 / 87 = 680	-23	3	22
Latin America	40 / 465 / 40 = 544	-19	1	21
North America	1 / 260 / 45 = 307	-54	-8	29

Legend: □ Basic ▨ Smart feature ■ Advanced operating system (OS)

NOTE: Numbers may not sum due to rounding.
SOURCE: Yankee Group; McKinsey Global Institute analysis

THERE ARE THREE MAIN CATEGORIES OF APPLICATIONS USING PERSONAL LOCATION DATA

We have identified three major categories of applications of personal location data. Location-based applications and services for individuals is a category that includes smart routing, automotive telematics, and mobile-phone based location services. The second category is the organizational use of individual personal location data that includes geo-targeted advertising, electronic toll collection, insurance pricing, and emergency response. Third is the macro-level use of aggregate location data that includes urban planning and retail business intelligence.

In this section, we will describe several examples of each type of application. However, this is such a dynamic field with such a high degree of change and innovation that our examples should not be regarded as exhaustive.

Location-based applications and services for individuals

1. **Smart routing.** Smart routing based on real-time traffic information is one of the most heavily used applications of personal location data.[78] The more advanced navigation systems can receive information about traffic in real time, including accidents, scheduled roadwork, and congested areas. These systems are also capable of giving users up-to-date information on points of interest and impending weather conditions. Some of these devices can not only provide drivers with recommendations on which routes to take to avoid congestion but also report back information on location and movement to a central server, allowing congestion to be measured even more accurately.

---

78 We regard navigation using real-time traffic data as a big data application because it requires the analysis of a large pool of data about current traffic congestion. "Traditional" navigation systems that do not use real-time traffic data are still quite common and can provide considerable benefit. For example, a proprietary NAVTEQ research project conducted in Germany has shown that drivers using navigation devices drive shorter distances and spend less time driving (including improving fuel efficiency by 12 percent).

As the penetration of smartphones increases, and free navigation applications are included in these devices, the use of smart routing is likely to grow. By 2020, more than 70 percent of mobile phones are expected to have GPS capability, up from 20 percent in 2010. In addition, the number of automobiles equipped with dashboard GPS devices will continue to grow.

All told, we estimate the potential global value of smart routing in the form of time and fuel savings will be about $500 billion by 2020. This is the equivalent of saving drivers 20 billion hours on the road, or 10 to 15 hours every year for each traveler, and about $150 billion on fuel consumption. These savings translate into an estimated reduction in carbon dioxide emissions of 380 million tonnes, or more than 5 percent a year.[79] These estimates assume adequate investment in the two main areas of developing digital maps and the availability of real-time traffic information. Digital map data are available today in most developed countries and are becoming increasingly commonplace in developing countries. For smart routing to be effective, these maps will have to be kept up to date, a particular challenge in emerging markets where road networks and infrastructure are constantly changing. Moreover, for the full capture of this potential value, growth in demand will be necessary to spur the required investment in technology infrastructure, including hardware and transmission towers that are necessary to enable access to real-time traffic information.

2. **Automotive telematics.** Over coming years, an increasing number of automobiles will be equipped with GPS and telematics (i.e., the ability to send and receive data) that can enable a range of personal safety and monitoring services. One example already on the market is General Motors' OnStar service, which transmits real-time vehicle location and diagnostic information to a central monitoring site. Systems such as this—which are analogous to remote health monitoring in the health care system—can alert drivers to when they need repairs or software upgrades, or can locate vehicles during emergencies (e.g., when air bags have been deployed or a vehicle has been reported as stolen).

3. **Mobile phone location-based services.** There is also a fast-developing and broadening range of other location-based services (LBS) provided on mobile phones. These services include safety-related applications for tracking children and other family members, or finding friends. Examples already in place today include Foursquare (more than 8 million users as of April 2011) and Loopt (more than 5 million users in April 2011). Loopt, founded in 2006 in Mountain View, California, is a downloadable application for smartphones that allows users to share real-time location information, status messages, and geo-tagged photos with a community of friends. Detailed maps that are available on all major US networks and from several applications stores show where friends are, what they are doing, and how to meet up with them. Loopt generates revenue primarily through geo-targeted advertisements and promotions.

There are also location-based mobile services that find points of interest and provide additional information on, for instance, the nearest dry cleaner or Chinese restaurant or the best locations from which to hail a cab in crowded cities. In future years, personal location data will enable mobile gaming such as scavenger hunts or military simulations based on the locations of players (Exhibit 29).

---

79 We use McKinsey's proprietary model to arrive at this estimate of projected global emissions from road transportation in 2020.

The revenue model for such mobile LBS applications will be a mix of free services and applications supported by advertising and other revenue, including sponsored links from restaurants, bars, and other points of interest. Some mobile applications will feature embedded advertising or require a onetime download fee or ongoing subscription. In combination, we estimate that the new value generated by such services could be $80 billion or more in 2020. Some of this value will accrue as revenue to mobile LBS service providers, but consumers using the services will obtain much of the total value generated if research into the consumer surplus generated by online services in general is a guide.[80]

Exhibit 29

Mobile location-based services (LBS) and applications have proliferated

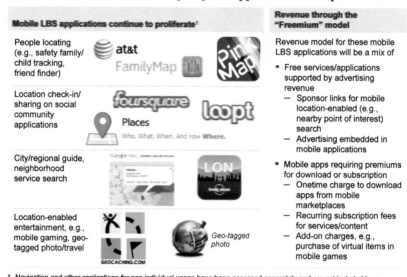

Mobile LBS applications continue to proliferate[1]

People locating (e.g., safety family/ child tracking, friend finder)

Location check-in/ sharing on social community applications

City/regional guide, neighborhood service search

Location-enabled entertainment, e.g., mobile gaming, geo-tagged photo/travel

Geo-tagged photo

Revenue through the "Freemium" model

Revenue model for these mobile LBS applications will be a mix of

- Free services/applications supported by advertising revenue
  - Sponsor links for mobile location-enabled (e.g., nearby point of interest) search
  - Advertising embedded in mobile applications
- Mobile apps requiring premiums for download or subscription
  - Onetime charge to download apps from mobile marketplaces
  - Recurring subscription fees for services/content
  - Add-on charges, e.g., purchase of virtual items in mobile games

1 Navigation and other applications for non-individual usage have been assessed separately and are not included here.
SOURCE: Press search; McKinsey Global Institute analysis

Organizational use of individual personal location data

1. **Geo-targeted advertising.** Geo-targeted mobile advertising is one of the most common ways organizations can create value from the use of personal location data. For example, consumers who choose to receive geo-targeted ads might have a personalized advertisement for a favorite store pop up on their smartphone when they are close to that store. Or a smartphone user meeting with friends at a bar or restaurant might receive a coupon offer for drinks or food from that establishment. This technology could direct users to the nearest ATM, provide location and time-based restaurant reviews, and offer a range of special offers for stores based on the smartphone user's location or destination. This type of advertising was still in its infancy in 2010. However, new geo-targeted advertising businesses such as ShopAlerts report impressive sales and response results (see Box 11, "ShopAlerts: Geo-targeted mobile ads"). Compared with more traditional forms of advertising such as TV or print, geo-targeted campaigns appear to have higher relevance to the consumer at the moment when a purchase decision is likely to be made and therefore boost the potential for an actual sale. Advertisers certainly seem to believe this to be the case, and they are paying increased rates for this service compared with advertising without geo-targeting.

80 Consumers driving the digital uptake: The economic value of online advertising-based services for consumers, McKinsey & Company for IAB Europe, September 2010.

Box 11. ShopAlerts: Geo-targeted mobile ads

ShopAlerts, developed by PlaceCast of San Francisco and New York, is a location-based "push SMS" product that companies including Starbucks, North Face, Sonic, REI, and American Eagle Outfitters are already using to drive traffic into their stores. Advertisers define a geographic boundary in which to send opted-in users a push SMS typically in the form of a promotion or advertisement to visit a particular store; in general, a user would receive no more than three such alerts a week. ShopAlerts claims 1 million users worldwide. In the United States, the company says it can locate more than 90 percent of the mobile phones in use nationwide. The company reports that 79 percent of consumers surveyed say that they are more likely to visit a store when they receive a relevant SMS; 65 percent of respondents said they made a purchase because of the message; and 73 percent said they would probably or definitely use the service in the future.

2. **Electronic toll collection.** Current electronic toll collections require specialized technology that incurs significant costs, but increasingly commonplace GPS-enabled mobile phones are likely to spur the development of a toll collection application that could reduce the overall costs of the system. As an illustration, a mobile phone could locate the vehicle and tollbooth, pay the toll, and charge it to the user's phone bill, eliminating the need for separate transponder devices and additional bill payment accounts.

3. **Insurance pricing.** The combination of personal location data and vehicle telematics has the potential to offer insurers more accurate and detailed data on individual behavior—for example, how individual policyholders drive their automobiles. Such information would allow insurers to price risk based on actual behavior rather than on aggregate demographic factors. Some claim that behavior-based insurance could even reduce claims costs because individuals behave in a less risky way when they know they are being monitored. This effect needs to be proved, but what seems certain is that rapidly improving technologies based on personal location data have the potential to help insurers develop other services to encourage safer driving. For instance, insurers could begin offering real-time alerts on traffic and weather conditions (as we have seen in the case of smart routing), high-risk parking areas, and changing speed limits.

4. **Emergency response.** The increasing availability of personal location data, real-time traffic, and GPS telematics clearly offers scope for faster and more effective response times by law enforcement officers, firefighters, and ambulance personnel. These technologies enable emergency service dispatchers to identify quickly the location of a person reporting an emergency, ensure that personnel can respond as rapidly as possible (through smart routing), and monitor their own safety in often dangerous environments.

Macro-level use of aggregate location data

Two quite disparate areas of decision making that can benefit from the analysis of personal location data in aggregate are urban planning and retail business intelligence, which we highlight here. However, we are confident that many other applications and business models will emerge as these technologies improve and their use proliferates.

1. **Urban planning.** Urban planners can benefit significantly from the analysis of personal location data. Decisions that can be improved by analyzing such data

92

include road and mass-transit construction, the mitigation of traffic congestion, and planning for high-density development. Urban transit and development planners will increasingly have access to a large amount of information about peak and off-peak traffic hotspots, volumes and patterns of transit use, and shopping trends, for instance—and in the process potentially cut congestion and the emission of pollutants. By drilling down into this wealth of data, urban planners will be more informed when they make decisions on anything from the placing and sequencing of traffic lights to the likely need for parking spaces. Singapore's public transportation department is already using ten-year demand forecasts partly based on personal location data to plan transit needs. Traffic agencies in the Netherlands are predicting traffic and pedestrian congestion using personal location data from mobile phones.

2. **Retail business intelligence.** Retailers can use personal location data to understand shopping patterns, aggregating information on foot-traffic density and speed to generate detailed insights about where shoppers slow down and speed up in response to promotions and advertising, and then linking these patterns with data on product purchases, customer demographics, and historical buying patterns. Such granular intelligence can help to improve a range of business decisions from in-store layout to merchandising (see Box 12, "How does tracking shoppers' movements work?").

Box 12. How does tracking shoppers' movements work?

Since GPS signals often do not penetrate indoors, retailers can use other electronic technologies to track shoppers as they move about within stores or shopping centers (Exhibit 30). These technologies include RFID tags on shopping carts, dedicated devices carried by customers, video cameras, and several innovative technologies leveraging mobile phones. Each of these techniques provides a different level of detail about location. RFID tags are cheap and accurate but often don't reflect shoppers detailed movements. For example, a tag can be attached to a cart that is left in an aisle while the consumer moves about. Video recognition can be excellent for the management of traffic flow but difficult to use for following an individual's behavior. Several technologies, including Shopkick and Path Intelligence (that we have already noted) are already on the market.

Exhibit 30

How does location tracking work?

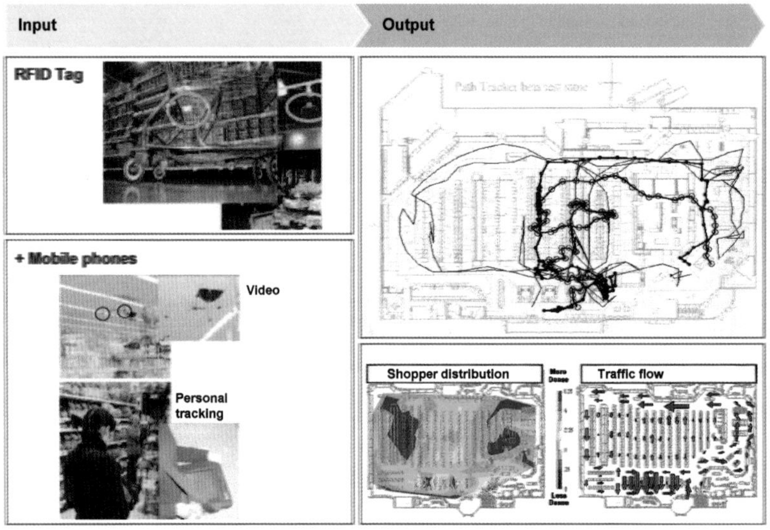

SOURCE: Press and literature search

3. **Some new business models.** As the availability of personal location data becomes more common and awareness of its value more widespread, other markets will develop for both aggregated and raw data. For example, Sense Networks is commercializing Macrosense, a machine-learning technology model that aggregates historical and real-time mobile phone location data to, for instance, identify the best street corners from which to hail a taxi (see Box 13, "Sense Networks: Analyzing aggregated location information"). As another example, the city of Boston has launched an application called Street Bump that takes advantage of personal location data to detect potholes. Street Bump uses technology already built into smartphones, including GPS and accelerometers, and notes the location of the car and the size of the potholes it crosses. The city has issued a public challenge to users to find the best methodology for mapping street conditions and making Street Bump as useful as possible.

Box 13. Sense Networks: Analyzing aggregated location information

Sense Networks, headquartered in New York City, was founded in 2003 by a team of computer scientists from the Massachusetts Institute of Technology and Columbia University. The company uses real-time and historical personal location data for predictive analytics. Sense Networks' first application for consumers was CitySense, a tool designed to answer the question: "Where is everyone going right now?" CitySense shows the overall activity level of the city, hotspots, and places with unexpectedly high activity, all in real time. The tool then links to Yelp and Google to show what venues are operating at those locations. CabSense, another Sense Network application released in early 2010, offers users an aggregated map generated by analyzing tens of millions of data points that ranks street corners by the number of taxicabs picking up passengers every hour or every day of the week.

THE VALUE CREATED BY PERSONAL LOCATION DATA IS SUBSTANTIAL AND GROWING

Our detailed analysis of the major applications of personal location data today and in the near future finds that, in ten years' time, these applications have the potential to create value of $100 billion or more for service providers alone. This additional value is likely to come primarily from sales of navigation hardware and revenue from LBS, mobile LBS premiums, and geo-targeted advertising.[81] Entrepreneurs will develop many of these services and applications, given the fact that the application store model for mobile devices is already providing ready sales and marketing channels, greatly lowering the barriers to entry for innovative new players.

The likely value that will accrue to providers will be dwarfed by the benefits that customers—both individuals and businesses—will enjoy because of proliferating location-based applications. We believe that by 2020, personal location applications will create as much as $700 billion in value for users (Exhibit 31). Of this, more than 70 percent will be the consumer surplus obtained from time and fuel saved by using GPS navigation systems (including those with real-time traffic information) and the use of mobile LBS applications (difference between willingness to pay and the cost

---

81 We have included navigation hardware sales because these devices are used exclusively for personal navigation applications. The number would be much larger if it included smartphone sales, which we exclude because smartphones are used for many purposes that do not require personal location data.

of applications). The remaining 30 percent of the total accruing to customers will be additional value obtained by businesses that make use of location data-enabled levers such as marketers' return on geo-targeted mobile advertising.

Exhibit 31

The value of the major levers increases to more than $800 billion by 2020

$ billion per annum

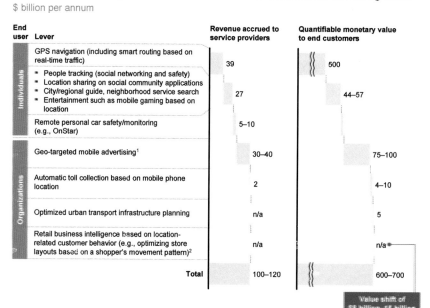

End user	Lever	Revenue accrued to service providers	Quantifiable monetary value to end customers
Individuals	GPS navigation (including smart routing based on real-time traffic)	39	500
Individuals	• People tracking (social networking and safety) • Location sharing on social community applications • City/regional guide, neighborhood service search • Entertainment such as mobile gaming based on location	27	44–57
Individuals	Remote personal car safety/monitoring (e.g., OnStar)	5–10	
Organizations	Geo-targeted mobile advertising[1]	30–40	75–100
Organizations	Automatic toll collection based on mobile phone location	2	4–10
Organizations	Optimized urban transport infrastructure planning	n/a	5
Organizations	Retail business intelligence based on location-related customer behavior (e.g., optimizing store layouts based on a shopper's movement pattern)[2]	n/a	n/a
	Total	100–120	600–700

Value shift of $5 billion–15 billion

1 For sizing the value of geo-targeted mobile advertising, service providers are defined as those that sell advertising inventory, e.g., advertising platform providers; customers are defined as the marketers who purchase advertising inventory.
2 Individual retailer will gain top-line increase, which represents a value shift rather than value creation at macro-level.
NOTE: Numbers may not sum due to rounding.
SOURCE: McKinsey Global Institute analysis

We believe that our estimates of the potential surplus that will accrue to customers are conservative because they do not include additional sources of utility such as improvements in user convenience, transparency, and entertainment. Personal location data-enabled services such as user ranking applications (e.g., Yelp) offer users all of these benefits. Unfamiliar travelers, for instance, can quickly find shops and eateries they might favor. Familiar residents can locate friends, the evening's most popular nightspots, and the shortest driving route. Furthermore, our estimates size the potential impact of only a few applications; we expect innovative new uses of personal location data and business models to continue to emerge. Creativity and innovation will shift the value potential upward from our present estimates, and a long tail of specialized applications will combine to offer substantial total additional value.

Individuals and organizations around the world will share in the potential value of personal location data—nowhere more dramatically than in emerging markets where the already very large number of mobile phones generating such data is increasing so rapidly..

A RANGE OF BARRIERS NEED TO BE OVERCOME TO REALIZE THE FULL VALUE OF PERSONAL LOCATION DATA

The creation of much of the potential value enabled by personal location data will depend on resolving a range of technological and other business issues and ameliorating institutional and government barriers. Some of these issues and barriers are familiar; others less so; some are more intractable than others. The challenges that business and policy makers face include privacy and security concerns, technology investment and innovation, and managing organizational change.

As the volume and accuracy of personal location data increases, so will concerns about privacy and security. Laws are generally unclear on which constituency—from mobile operators, platform owners, application developers, and handset manufacturers, to actual users—owns the right to collect, aggregate, disseminate, and use personal location data for commercial purposes. Many commercial enterprises that state they will protect the privacy of these data have been able to use them relatively freely. But there are calls from citizens who want to know that their privacy and the security of their personal location data are protected and who believe that opt-in/opt-out agreements are unclear. A framework that clearly describes the permissible and prohibited use of these data would be beneficial for all stakeholders.

It seems inevitable that the technology related to personal location data will continue to improve as market demand intensifies and mobile devices become ubiquitous around the world. Our projections for the value that these data will create assume continuing technological innovation (e.g., Moore's Law increasing the capabilities of semiconductors) and infrastructure investment (e.g., in upgraded cell phone base stations for higher bandwidth), and the widespread adoption of GPS-enabled mobile devices. Although current civil GPS accuracy appears to be adequate for many existing applications, other applications will require more fine-grained location data, such as inside buildings.

And there will be technological challenges. For instance, operators of developing applications will have to be alert to the possibility of novel complications and errors. The Dutch government, collecting and analyzing highway congestion data based on the density of mobile phone positions, observed that a particular segment of highway had a curious congestion peak that appeared and disappeared abruptly every hour. It transpired that the highway was close to a commuter rail line with a train passing at peak times on the hour.

All of these aspects of the evolving personal location data domain pose significant challenges for executives and policy makers. Business leaders should already be considering the potential benefits of leveraging these data, particularly in the areas of marketing and improving operational efficiencies, and building business cases around today's perceptible opportunities. But they should also experiment with new business models to derive the maximum value. Executives should work in the common interest with public policy makers to craft effective privacy policies, the means to communicate them clearly to the public, and to enhance the security of information around personal location data. The private and public sectors can also collaborate on accelerating the development and adoption of infrastructure and devices that have the potential to generate additional useful personal location data.

For policy makers, the first priority in this rapidly developing domain is to ensure that appropriate incentives for innovation are in place including developing an up-to-date framework for intellectual property rules and rights, funding R&D in potential breakthrough areas, and ensuring that the infrastructure, including spectrum policies, is optimal.

□ □ □

Applying personal location data has the potential to provide more than $800 billion in economic value to individual consumers and organizations over the next decade, in the process catalyzing the development of a wide range of innovative businesses across many sectors. Smart navigation applications alone may offer some $500 billion in value to global consumers in time and fuel saved by 2020. Geo-targeted advertising is emerging as a highly effective marketing vehicle that could represent more than 5 percent of total global advertising spending by 2020. Executives and policy makers need to work together to enable the growth of this data domain and unleash its full potential.

4. Key findings that apply across sectors

The use of big data offers tremendous untapped potential for creating value. Organizations in many industry sectors and business functions can leverage big data to improve their allocation and coordination of human and physical resources, cut waste, increase transparency and accountability, and facilitate the discovery of new ideas and insights. In addition to the five domains we studied in depth, we also found many other examples in other domains, across geographies, of the tremendous potential to create value from the use of big data. In this chapter, we synthesize what we have learned from the five domains we studied in depth as well as our observations in other domains.

BIG DATA CREATES VALUE IN SEVERAL WAYS

We have identified five broadly applicable ways to leverage big data that offer transformational potential to create value, and have implications for how individual organizations will have to be designed, organized, and managed. Questions that these findings raise include: How will corporate marketing functions and activities need to evolve if large-scale experimentation is possible and how are business processes likely to change? How will companies value and leverage their assets (particularly data assets) and could their access to, and analysis of, data actually generate more value than, say, a brand? How might big data disrupt established business models? For example, some industry dynamics rest on the fact that there are information asymmetries—how would those dynamics change if transparency around data produced information symmetry instead? How will incumbents with legacy business models and infrastructures compete with newcomers that do not face such constraints? And what will the world look like when surplus starts shifting from suppliers to customers?

1. Creating transparency

Making big data more easily accessible to relevant stakeholders in a timely way can create tremendous value. Indeed, this aspect of creating value is a prerequisite for all other levers and is the most immediate way for businesses and sectors that are today less advanced in embracing big data and its levers to capture that potential. In many cases, these opportunities exist where there is a misalignment of incentives for creating data transparency, such as lack of a performance imperative. For example, in the public sector, we discovered cases where departmental personnel were spending 20 percent of their time searching for information from other government departments using non-digital means (e.g., paper directories and calling people), and then obtaining that information by traveling to other locations and picking up data on physical media such as compact disks. Such wasted effort has been greatly reduced in organizations that have harnessed big data to digitize that information, make it available through networks, and deploy search tools to make relevant information easier to find.

However, even in sectors that have embraced IT and big data and where there are considerable incentives for higher performance, we found room for increasing transparency and the sharing of big data. In manufacturing, many companies have used big data to improve performance in R&D (e.g., complex simulations) or in the management of their supply chains. However, these applications often take advantage of only those data that are contained within a single functional group in a company. Integrating data from R&D, engineering, and manufacturing units, potentially across several enterprises, can enable concurrent engineering techniques that can greatly reduce the waste caused from having to rework designs, and thus accelerate time to market.

2. Enabling experimentation to discover needs, expose variability, and improve performance

The ability for organizations to instrument—to deploy technology that allows them to collect data—and sense the world is continually improving. More and more companies are digitizing and storing an increasing amount of highly detailed data about transactions. More and more sensors are being embedded in physical devices—from assembly-line equipment to automobiles to mobile phones—that measure processes, the use of end products, and human behavior. Individual consumers, too, are creating and sharing a tremendous amount of data through blogging, status updates, and posting photos and videos. Much of these data can now be collected in real or near real time.

Having access to all of these data and in some cases being able to manipulate the conditions under which they are generated enable a very different way of making decisions that involves bringing more science into management—i.e., applying classic scientific methods to the practice of management.[82] Specifically, managers now can use a scientific process of controlled experimentation that includes the formulation of specific hypotheses, designing and conducting experiments (including control and treatment groups) to test those hypotheses, and then rigorously analyzing the quantitative results before making a decision. Many companies make decisions in a highly ad hoc way—as some have put it, through "management by HiPPOs, the Highest Paid Person's Opinions."[83] A data-driven organization makes decisions on the basis of the empirical results, and the benefits of such an approach toward data have been demonstrated by academic research.[84]

Leaders in many sectors are already beginning to use controlled experiments to make better decisions. For instance, the health care sector now conducts comparative effectiveness studies on population-wide clinical data to identify and understand the sources of variability in treatments and outcomes, identify treatment protocols that are most effective and efficient, and help decision makers to create guidelines designed to ensure that treatment decisions are based on the best science. Retailers, especially those that operate online but increasingly also those with physical stores, are adjusting prices and promotions in a bid to experiment with which combination best drives traffic and sales.

It isn't always possible (perhaps for ethical reasons or feasibility) to set up a controlled experiment to manipulate an independent variable. An alternative is seek out "natural experiments" to identify existing variability in performance metrics. Understanding the drivers of this naturally occurring variability can then be used to guide

---

82 Janaki Akella, Timo Kubach, Markus Löffler, and Uwe Schmid, *Data-driven management: Bringing more science into management*, McKinsey Technology Initiative Perspective, 2008.

83 The earliest reference we have to this acronym was by Google analytics evangelist Avinash Kaushik. See *Seven steps to creating a data driven decision making culture*, October 2006 (www.kaushik.net/avinash/2006/10/seven-steps-to-creating-a-data-driven-decision-making-culture.html).

84 Erik Brynjolfsson, Lorin M. Hitt, and Heekyung Hellen Kim, *Strength in numbers: How does data-driven decisionmaking affect firm performance?*, April 2011, available at SSRN (ssrn.com/abstract=1819486).

management levers to improve that performance. In the public sector, we found large agencies that discovered huge variations in the productivity and accuracy of work at different sites performing nearly identical tasks. Simply making this information available across sites had the effect of spurring locations that were lagging to improve their performance significantly. No changes in compensation were promised; once people knew they were underperforming, their competitive nature kicked in and their observing best practices in the top-performing sites helped to transform their performance without monetary incentives.

3. Segmenting populations to customize actions

Targeting services or marketing to meet individual needs is already familiar to consumer-facing companies. For them, the idea of segmenting and analyzing their customers through combinations of attributes such as demographics, customer purchase metrics, and shopping attitudes and behavior is firmly established. Companies such as insurance companies and credit card issuers that rely on risk judgments have also long used big data to segment customers. However, as technology improves, many companies have been able to segment and analyze in near real time. Even in the public sector that tends to treat all constituencies the same, using big data to segment is catching on. For instance, some public labor agencies have used big data to tailor job training services for different segments of job seekers, the aim being to ensure that the most efficient and effective interventions are applied to get different people back to work. Another example from the public sector is tax agencies that segment taxpayers by a range of factors including income, past delinquent rate, and credit history to identify returns that are most appropriate for further audits.

4. Replacing/supporting human decision making with automated algorithms

Sophisticated analytics can substantially improve decision making, minimize risks, and unearth valuable insights that would otherwise remain hidden. Big data either provides the raw material needed to develop algorithms or for those algorithms to operate. Best practice tax agencies, for instance, use automated risk engines that use big data to flag candidates for further examination. Big data algorithms in retail can optimize decision processes, enabling the automatic fine tuning of inventories and pricing in response to real time in-store and online sales. Manufacturing companies can adjust production lines automatically to optimize efficiency, reduce waste, and avoid dangerous conditions. In some cases, companies will not necessarily automate decisions but facilitate them by analyzing datasets that are far larger than those data pools that are manageable for an individual using a spreadsheet. Some organizations are already making more effective decisions by analyzing entire datasets from customers and employees, or even from sensors embedded in products. Big-data-based analytics today include rule-based systems, statistical analyses, and machine-learning techniques such as neural networks. This is a fast-moving area, and new forms of data-based analytics are being developed all the time. (See chapter on "Big data techniques and technologies.")

5. Innovating new business models, products and services

Big data enables enterprises of all kinds to create new products and services, enhance existing ones, and invent entirely new business models. In health care, analyzing patient clinical and behavior data has created preventive care programs targeting the most appropriate groups of individuals. Castlight Health is a company that analyzes big data to make available to patients in large health plans data on health care pricing that they don't normally see. Ingenix in the health care sector and

100

Nielsen in retail specialize in the aggregation and analysis of various datasets for institutions. Also in retailing, real-time price comparison services give consumers price transparency to a degree never before enjoyed and generate significant surplus for them. Manufacturers are using data obtained from sensors embedded in products to create innovative after-sales service offerings such as proactive maintenance (preventive measures that take place before a failure occurs or is even noticed) and as the basis for the development of next generations of products. The emergence of real-time location data has created an entirely new suite of location-based mobile services from navigation applications to people tracking.

WHILE THE USE OF BIG DATA WILL MATTER ACROSS SECTORS, SOME SECTORS ARE POISED FOR GREATER GAINS

Using a value potential index that combines several quantitative metrics, we compared the historical productivity of sectors in the United States with the potential of these sectors to capture value from big data.[85] We observed that patterns vary from sector to sector (Exhibit 32).[86]

Exhibit 32

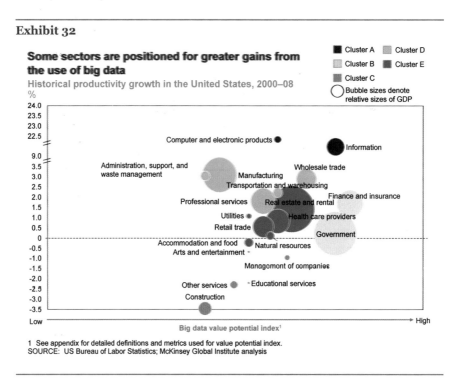

Some sectors are positioned for greater gains from the use of big data

Historical productivity growth in the United States, 2000–08

1 See appendix for detailed definitions and metrics used for value potential index.
SOURCE: US Bureau of Labor Statistics; McKinsey Global Institute analysis

Globally traded computer and electronic products and information sectors (Cluster A) are sectors that have already posted very strong productivity growth and are set to gain substantially from using big data. These sectors have access to huge pools of data (e.g., Internet companies collect vast amounts of online behavior data) and the pace of

85 We studied the United States because of the relative availability of relevant data, particularly around the numbers and sizes of individual firms. The applicability of these specific findings in other geographies will vary based on the similarities of individual sectors.

86 The value potential index consists of five metrics that are designed as proxies to indicate (1) the amount of data available for use and analysis; (2) variability in performance; (3) number of stakeholders (customers and suppliers) with which an organization deals on average; (4) transaction intensity; and (5) turbulence inherent in a sector. We believe that these are the characteristics that make a sector more or less likely to take advantage of the five transformative big data opportunities. See the appendix for further details.

innovation is very high (e.g., rapid product introductions in consumer electronics). Even in the near term, we see significant scope to capture more value from big data.

Two services sectors (Cluster B)—finance & insurance and government—are positioned to benefit very strongly from big data as long as barriers to its use can be overcome. These sectors are both transaction- and customer-intensive, suggesting that they can increase their application of levers involving segmentation and automated algorithms. They both also have high degrees of variability in their performance, suggesting that they could use data and experimentation to improve performance.

Several sectors (Cluster C) including construction, educational services, and arts and entertainment, have posted negative productivity growth, which probably indicates that these sectors face strong systemic barriers to increasing productivity. Nevertheless, if those barriers can be overcome, we think that big data can enable productivity increases even in these sectors. Examples of where potential exists include measuring variations in the performance of teachers in improving the academic achievement of students—teacher value added—that can be an effective tool for helping to increase productivity in education.

Among the remaining sectors, globally traded sectors (mostly Cluster D) (e.g., manufacturing, wholesale trade) tend to have experienced higher historical productivity growth, while local services (mainly Cluster E) (e.g., retail, health care providers, accommodation and food) have achieved lower growth. Many of these sectors can derive significant value from big data, although doing so will depend on the extent to which barriers are overcome. Sectors that may have more moderate potential from the use of big data, such as construction and administrative services, tend not to have characteristics that could make exploiting big data opportunities more challenging than in other sectors.. They have less data than other sectors and fewer stakeholders, and are also less transaction-intensive.

Our index indicates that of the sectors that we studied in detail, two—health care and manufacturing—appear to have only modest potential from the use of big data. This is because the index measures several criteria at the level of the individual firm (e.g., amount of data per firm as a proxy for number of customers per firm). In the United States, for instance, both of these industries are highly fragmented—they have many more firms or players than other sectors. Given that data are usually fragmented along firm or organizational boundaries, this implies that big data opportunities will be limited across these sectors. Nevertheless, even in these industries, large-scale players have the ability to aggregate enough data to derive significant value (see chapter 3a on health care for examples). Furthermore, it is possible, albeit usually more challenging, for many individual firms to pool, share, or trade data, sometimes through third parties, in order to capture value from big data (see, in particular, chapter 3d on manufacturing, where global distributed supply chains can be optimized by sharing big data). Consolidation in an industry can also bring about beneficial scale effects in the aggregation and analysis of data.

While all sectors will have to overcome barriers to capture value from the use of big data, barriers are structurally higher for some than for others (Exhibit 33). For example, government may face higher hurdles because of challenges around data availability and data-driven mind-sets. Education faces similar challenges, along with a relative lack of investment in IT. Moreover, the competitive intensity in these sectors is relatively low compared with those sectors where market forces work more freely. In more market-driven sectors, the imperative to leverage data is strengthened by more direct links to economic value for the firms and users involved. Sectors such as finance & insurance, manufacturing, and professional services may have relatively lower degrees of barriers to overcome for precisely the opposite reasons.

Exhibit 33

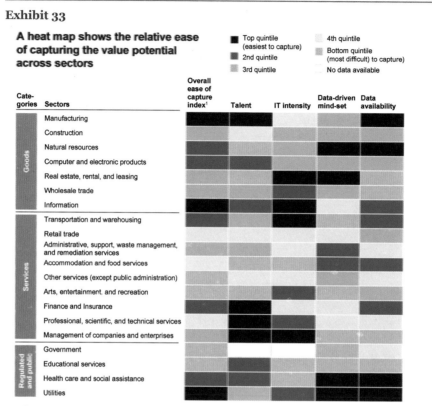

A heat map shows the relative ease of capturing the value potential across sectors

■ Top quintile (easiest to capture) ▢ 4th quintile
▣ 2nd quintile ▢ Bottom quintile (most difficult) to capture)
▨ 3rd quintile No data available

Categories	Sectors	Overall ease of capture index[1]	Talent	IT intensity	Data-driven mind-set	Data availability
Goods	Manufacturing					
	Construction					
	Natural resources					
	Computer and electronic products					
	Real estate, rental, and leasing					
	Wholesale trade					
	Information					
Services	Transportation and warehousing					
	Retail trade					
	Administrative, support, waste management, and remediation services					
	Accommodation and food services					
	Other services (except public administration)					
	Arts, entertainment, and recreation					
	Finance and Insurance					
	Professional, scientific, and technical services					
	Management of companies and enterprises					
Regulated and public	Government					
	Educational services					
	Health care and social assistance					
	Utilities					

1 See appendix for detailed definitions and metrics used for each of the criteria.
SOURCE: McKinsey Global Institute analysis

BIG DATA OFFERS VERY LARGE POTENTIAL TO GENERATE VALUE GLOBALLY, BUT SOME GEOGRAPHIES COULD GAIN FIRST

Our five case studies covered both developed and emerging economies and our findings suggest that the use of big data can drive significant value across geographies. We found very significant potential to create value in developed markets by applying big data levers in health care and retail. However, if we take the time savings for drivers achievable from using navigation tools in the personal location data domain, we find that 20 to 40 percent of the global potential is in emerging markets.

Different economies and regions exhibit very different characteristics from the amount of data they generate to the maturity of their ICT infrastructure. This indicates that some geographies might be poised to capture value more quickly than others. Access to big data is a key prerequisite to capturing value. Today, North America and Europe account for the majority of new data stored (Exhibit 34). This suggests that, in the near term at least, much of the global potential to create value through the use of big data will be in the most developed economies. Although this may be true in aggregate, individual firms in emerging markets could enjoy access to big data that could enable them to capture significant value. In addition, organizations in developing markets could store and analyze their data in data centers located in developed markets.

As long as the right conditions are in place, there is significant potential to leverage big data in developing economies. Consider the fact that Asia is already the leading region for the generation of personal location data simply because so many mobile phones are in use. More mobile phones—an estimated 800 million devices in 2010—are in use in China than in any other country (see Exhibit 28). Furthermore, although some emerging market organizations lag behind their counterparts in developed market in terms of IT assets, this could actually prove to be an advantage. Organizations in developing economies could leapfrog to the latest technology, by-passing the legacy systems with which many of their counterparts in advanced economies have to grapple.

Exhibit 34

Amount of new data stored varies across geography

New data stored[1] by geography, 2010
Petabytes

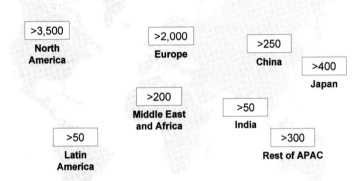

1 New data stored defined as the amount of available storage used in a given year; see appendix for more on the definition and assumptions.
SOURCE: IDC storage reports; McKinsey Global Institute analysis

THERE WILL BE A SHORTAGE OF THE TALENT ORGANIZATIONS NEED TO TAKE ADVANTAGE OF BIG DATA

A shortage of people with the skills necessary to take advantage of the insights that large datasets generate is one of the most important constraints on an organization's ability to capture the potential from big data. Leading companies are already reporting challenges in hiring this type of talent. Google's chief economist Hal Varian has been reported as saying that "the sexy job of the next ten years will be statisticians."[87]

Our research identifies three key types of talent required to capture value from big data: deep analytical talent—people with technical skills in statistics and machine learning, for example, who are capable of analyzing large volumes of data to derive business insights; data-savvy managers and analysts who have the skills to be effective consumers of big data insights—i.e., capable of posing the right questions for analysis, interpreting and challenging the results, and making appropriate decisions; and supporting technology personnel who develop, implement, and maintain the hardware and software tools such as databases and analytic programs needed to make use of big data. We expect the supply of talent in all of these categories to be a significant constraint on the ability of organizations around the

---

87 Steve Lohr, "For today's graduate, just one word: Statistics," *New York Times*, August 5, 2009.

world to capture value from big data, with the most acute needs in the first and second categories.[88] Given the amount of data on talent readily available, we used the US labor market to test this hypothesis.[89]

The US labor market has historically had a high level of graduates with degrees in the so-called STEM fields: science, technology, engineering, and mathematics. However, in recent years, the supply of such graduates has been sluggish at a time when demand for them has been rising. For example, at the peak of the last US economic expansion, employment for mathematics-related occupations increased by almost 4 percent and their real wages increased 1 percent; at this time national employment increased by only 1.5 percent and real wages rose by only 0.6 percent.[90] During this period, the number of advanced degrees conferred in math, statistics, and engineering declined by around 2 percent. In the future, the need for talent able to deal with big data will, in fact, be much more specific than simply STEM graduates. For this reason, we conducted a detailed analysis comparing potential demand for the first two categories of big data talent—deep analytical talent and data-savvy managers and analysts—with projected supply on current trends.

In the case of deep analytical talent, we used US Bureau of Labor Statistics (BLS) data on current occupations to analyze the supply of talent in the US workforce. The data were from 2008, the latest year for which complete data are available. We used existing BLS models to project the supply of deep analytical talent in 2018, assuming current trends hold.

We then used two separate analytical models to triangulate a perspective on the potential demand for deep analytical talent, assuming that companies across the economy fully adopt big data techniques by 2018. We based the first of these two models on an adaptation of the BLS model to account for varying degrees of growth in deep analytical talent based on the data intensity of different companies. We based the second model on the required numbers of deep analytic talent in different industries according to company size.

We estimate that the supply in the United States of deep analytical talent in 2008 was around 150,000 positions. If we take into account current trends in new graduates with deep analytical training (e.g., people taking graduate courses in statistics or machine learning, a subspecialty of computer science, or students taking such courses designed for their last year of undergraduate education) and immigration, this total rises to about 300,000. However, in a big data world, we expect demand for deep analytical talent could reach 440,000 to 490,000 positions in 2018—that's a talent gap in this category alone of 140,000 to 190,000 positions. In short, the United States will need an additional supply of this class of talent of 50 to 60 percent (Exhibit 35). Developing deep analytical skills requires an intrinsic aptitude in mathematics for starters, and then takes years of training. Addressing the talent shortage will not happen overnight, and the search for deep analytical talent that has already begun can only intensify.

88 We also did not prioritize the analysis of the supporting IT talent because other researchers have researched and debated this issue extensively.

89 In general, we found detailed occupational data on categories of knowledge workers to be relatively scarce outside the United States. See chapter on "Implications for policy makers" for a recommendation that more detailed data on these categories be collected.

90 Standard Occupational Classification (SOC) 15: Computer and mathematical occupations as defined by the US Bureau of Labor Statistics.

Exhibit 35

The United States graduates the largest number of people with deep analytical training

Number of graduates with deep analytical training in 2008[1]

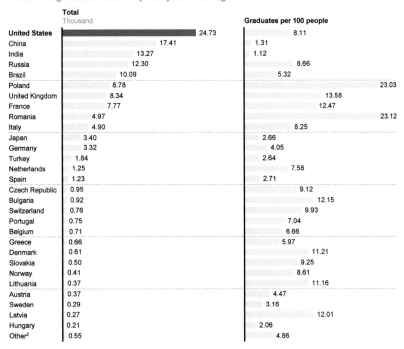

	Total Thousand	Graduates per 100 people
United States	24.73	8.11
China	17.41	1.31
India	13.27	1.12
Russia	12.30	8.66
Brazil	10.09	5.32
Poland	8.78	23.03
United Kingdom	8.34	13.58
France	7.77	12.47
Romania	4.97	23.12
Italy	4.90	8.25
Japan	3.40	2.66
Germany	3.32	4.05
Turkey	1.84	2.64
Netherlands	1.25	7.58
Spain	1.23	2.71
Czech Republic	0.95	9.12
Bulgaria	0.92	12.15
Switzerland	0.76	9.93
Portugal	0.75	7.04
Belgium	0.71	6.66
Greece	0.66	5.97
Denmark	0.61	11.21
Slovakia	0.50	9.25
Norway	0.41	8.61
Lithuania	0.37	11.16
Austria	0.37	4.47
Sweden	0.29	3.16
Latvia	0.27	12.01
Hungary	0.21	2.06
Other[2]	0.55	4.86

1 These data count new graduates, i.e., a flow of deep analytical talent, which we define as people with advanced training in statistics and/or machine learning and who conduct data analysis.
2 Other includes Finland, Estonia, Croatia, Slovenia, Iceland, Cyprus, Macedonia, and Malta.
SOURCE: Eurostat; Russia Statistics; Japan Ministry of Education; India Sat; NASSCOM Strategic Review 2005; China Statistical Yearbook; China Education News; IMF World Economic Outlook Database

Although we conducted this analysis in the United States, we believe that the shortage of deep analytical talent will be a global phenomenon. There are significant variations, however, both in gross and per capita terms, in the number of graduates with these skills that different countries are producing. Countries with a higher per capita production of deep analytical talent could potentially be attractive sources of these skills for other geographies either through immigration or through companies offshoring to meet their needs (Exhibits 36 and 37).

In the case of data-savvy managers and analysts in a big data world, the level of training and mathematical aptitude is much lower than that required for deep analytical talent. People in these roles simply need enough conceptual knowledge and quantitative skills to be able to frame and interpret analyses in an effective way. It is possible to develop such skills through a single course in statistics and experimental design. However, managers and analysts will be necessary in every sector. We applied a methodology similar to that used to analyze deep analytical talent to understand the potential gap between projected demand and supply. By 2018, in the United States, we estimate that 4 million positions will require these types of skills in a big data world. However, if we add together the number of people with these skills and new graduates who will enter the market (on current trends), we reach a total of only 2.5 million people in the United States in 2018. So there is a potential shortfall of 1.5 million data-savvy managers and analysts. This is not a gap likely to be filled simply by changing graduate requirements and waiting for people to graduate with enhanced skills or importing talent (although these could be important actions to take). Thus, retraining the existing workforce will be necessary.

Exhibit 36

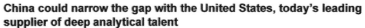

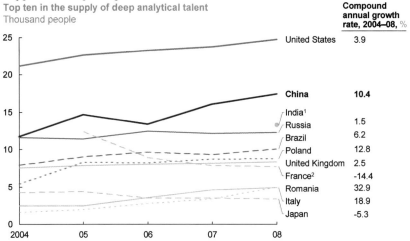

China could narrow the gap with the United States, today's leading supplier of deep analytical talent

Top ten in the supply of deep analytical talent
Thousand people

	Compound annual growth rate, 2004–08, %
United States	3.9
China	10.4
India[1]	
Russia	1.5
Brazil	6.2
Poland	12.8
United Kingdom	2.5
France[2]	-14.4
Romania	32.9
Italy	18.9
Japan	-5.3

1 India ranked third in 2008 with 13,270 people with deep analytical skills but India does not have a time series for these data.
2 For France, the compound annual growth rate is for 2005 and 2008 because of data availability.
SOURCE: Eurostat; national statistical agencies; Japan Ministry of Education; India Sat; NASSCOM; China Statistical Yearbook; China *Education News*, April 2005; IMF *World Economic Outlook*; McKinsey Global Institute analysis

---

Exhibit 37

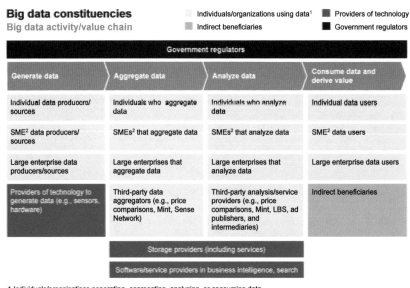

Big data constituencies
Big data activity/value chain

1 Individuals/organizations generating, aggregating, analyzing, or consuming data.
2 Small and medium-sized enterprises.
SOURCE: McKinsey Global Institute analysis

SEVERAL ISSUES WILL HAVE TO BE ADDRESSED TO CAPTURE THE FULL POTENTIAL OF BIG DATA

Data policies

As an ever larger amount of data is digitized and travels across organizational boundaries, there are a set of policy issues that will become increasingly important, including, but not limited to, privacy, security, intellectual property, and even liability.[91]

More information than ever is known about individuals, including sensitive data such as health and financial records, and many citizens will demand that companies and their governments to protect their privacy. Personal data such as health and financial records are often those that can offer the most significant human benefits, such as helping to pinpoint the right medical treatment, or the most appropriate financial product. However, consumers also view these categories of data as being the most sensitive. Individuals, companies, and governments will need to be thoughtful about the trade-offs between privacy and utility.

We are already seeing data security becoming a more pressing issue now that data are a key factor of production and a competitive asset. One study found that the number of compromised records increased by 30 percent each year between 2005 and 2009 in the United States.[92] Another study found that security compromises cost more than $200 per record in detection, notification, and remediation efforts, as well as customers lost.[93] Such security breaches affect a range of sectors including financial institutions, retail, hotels, and even national defense.

Big data's increasing economic importance also raises a number of legal issues, especially when coupled with the fact that data are fundamentally different from many other assets. Data can be copied perfectly and easily combined with other data, and the same piece of data can be used simultaneously by more than one person. So, intellectual property will become an even more important consideration for policy makers, who will set the rules that determine the legal rights associated with the ownership and use of data, and what constitutes "fair use" of data. Liability— such as who is responsible when an inaccurate piece of data leads to negative consequences—is another issue likely to come to the fore.

Technology and techniques

Today, legacy systems and incompatible standards and formats today often prevent the integration of data and the more sophisticated analytics that create value from big data. Organizations will need to deploy new technologies and techniques as they develop to overcome this barrier. Ultimately, making use of large digital datasets will require the assembly of a technology stack from storage and computing through analytical and visualization software applications. The specific technology requirements and priorities will vary based on the big data levers that are to be implemented and the data maturity of an institution, leading to very different levels of investment costs. Some companies lack the technology to capture data digitally in the first place (e.g., some smaller US health care provider practices) or to extract, transform, and load large datasets from other sources. Other organizations will need to supplement their existing storage or computing resources. Many will

---

91 Data privacy and security are important and pervasive concerns, which are being studied and debated at great length elsewhere, but have not been the major focus of the research in this report.

92 *The leaking vault: Five years of data breaches*, Digital Forensics Association, July 2010.

93 *Fourth annual US cost of data breach study*, Ponemon Institute, January 2009.

need to implement advanced analytical and visualization software tools. In many cases, legacy systems and incompatible standards and formats will have to be taken into account. Examples include joining different data pools as we might see at financial services companies that want to combine online financial transaction data, the behavior of customers in branches, data from partners such as insurance companies, and retail purchase history. Also, many levers require a tremendous scale of data (e.g., merging patient records across multiple providers), which can put unique demands upon technology infrastructures. To provide a framework under which to develop and manage the many interlocking technology components necessary to successfully execute big data levers, each organization will need to craft and execute a robust enterprise data strategy.

Organizational change and talent

Organizational leaders need to understand that big data can unlock value—and how to use it to that effect. It is vital that organizations learn how to leverage big data if they don't know how to already—because many of their rivals will certainly be using big data to carve out competitive advantage. As we have noted, many organizations neither have the skilled personnel they need to mine big data for insights nor the structures and incentives required to use big data to make more informed decisions and act on them.

Access to data

Access to data will need to broaden to capture the full potential for value creation. Increasingly, companies will need to acquire access to third-party data sources and integrate external information with their own, to capture the full potential of big data. In many cases, efficient markets are yet to be set up for trading or sharing data. For example, there are no efficient markets for the sharing of aggregate movement patterns derived from mobile phones—potentially valuable to retailers trying to understand consumer behavior. In other cases, incentives are misaligned so that stakeholders want to keep the information to themselves. In health care, for instance, providers will need to make a large big data investment to create, aggregate and analyze digital clinical data from medical records, which may reveal information that payors will use to their advantage in contract negotiations (e.g., payors direct patients away from providers with high cost but average performance). In order to fully capture the value that can be enabled by big data, the barriers to accessing data will have to be overcome.

Industry structure

The relative ease—of difficulty—of capturing value from big data will sometimes depend on the structure of a particular sector or industry. Sectors with a relative lack of competitive intensity and performance transparency and industries with highly concentrated profit pools are likely to be slow to fully leverage the benefits of big data. The public sector, for example, tends to have limited competitive pressure, which limits efficiency and productivity and puts a higher barrier up against the capture of value from using big data. US health care not only has a lack of transparency in terms of the cost and quality of treatment but also an industry structure in which payors gain from the use of clinical data (e.g., from fewer payouts for unnecessary treatment) but at the expense of the providers (e.g., fewer medical activities to charge for) from whom they would have to obtain those clinical data. As these examples suggest, organization leaders and policy makers need to consider how industry structures could evolve in a big data world if they are to determine how to optimize value creation in firms, sectors, and economies as a whole.

□ □ □

Our research suggests that there is a range of ways that big data can create value that companies and organizations, including governments, can apply across sectors. But to do so with maximum effectiveness will require all these players to overcome a range of barriers and to address key issues that are of deep concern to the public, notably privacy and security. In the next two chapters, we will discuss what companies, organizations, and policy makers can do to ease the path toward the full capture of the value that big data can create.

5. Implications for organization leaders

As big data and its levers become an increasingly valuable asset, their intelligent exploitation will be critical for enterprises to compete effectively. We already see organizations that understand and embrace the use of big data pulling ahead of their peers in tangible corporate performance measures. The use of big data will become a key basis of competition across sectors, so it is imperative that organizational leaders begin to incorporate big data into their business plans.

While the particular opportunities to leverage big data to create value will differ by sectors, as we have demonstrated in our domain case studies, organization leaders can start identifying and assessing the opportunities along the five cross-cutting themes we have identified. In addition, there is a set of common enablers that each executive should address in order to unlock the power of big data. Organizations will not only need to ensure that they have sufficient skills in back-office analytics but also manage a transition toward the right managerial talent on the front line that will be capable of executing strategy based on the insights analysts mine from big data.

1. INVENTORY DATA ASSETS: PROPRIETARY, PUBLIC, AND PURCHASED

With data becoming a key competitive asset, leaders must understand the assets that they hold or to which they could have access. Organizations should conduct an inventory of their own proprietary data, and also systematically catalog other data to which they could potentially gain access, including publicly available data (e.g., government data, other data that are released into the public domain), and data that can be purchased (e.g., from data aggregators or other players in a data value chain).

Indeed, to enable transformative opportunities, companies will increasingly need to acquire access to third-party data sources, integrating such information with their own. In some cases, organizations will be able to purchase access to the data. In other cases, the sources of third-party data might not have considered sharing it. Organizations will need to thoughtfully consider and present a compelling value proposition for these third parties to share or sell data to them, or determine another set of incentives (e.g., regulatory action) to ensure data access. A set of technology challenges (e.g., standardizing data, implementing data feeds) will often have to be addressed to ensure consistent, reliable, and timely access to external data.

For example, many companies have recently discovered the value of data from social media. Telecom companies have found that some information from social networks is useful in predicting customer churn. They discovered that customers who know others who have stopped using a certain telecom are more likely to do so themselves, so these likely-to-churn customers are then targeted for retention programs. Other consumer-facing companies have found that they can learn about customers' attitudes, buying trends, and taste from sentiments expressed online, allowing them to make timely changes in their marketing, and going forward changes in their product planning.

2. IDENTIFY POTENTIAL VALUE CREATION OPPORTUNITIES AND THREATS

We have described five cross-cutting categories of value creation through leveraging big data that can be applied across every function. Organizations should begin a process of identifying and prioritizing these opportunities; business line and function leaders should kick off processes in their respective areas of responsibility. It is worthwhile noting that identifying opportunities and potential sources of valuable data (see previous section), especially external sources of data, will often be an iterative, rather than sequential, process.

In order to validate these big data opportunities, leading organizations have often discovered that adopting a process of purposeful experimentation (a meta-application of the big data lever of experimentation) can be the most powerful path toward becoming an organization that fully leverages big data, rather that specifying a complete plan for the enterprise prior to doing any implementation. Selecting a few high-potential areas in which to experiment with big data, e.g., with digital marketing, and then rapidly scaling successes can be an effective way to begin the transformation.

In our research, we find that creating substantial new value does not necessarily require jumping directly to complex analytical big data levers. In many cases, the levers focused primarily on making data available or applying basic analytics can create substantial value even before an organization adopts more advanced levers. We see this in health care, where creating transparency and applying basic levers can generate about 40 percent of the value creation potential alone. Indeed, we find that most organizations follow a journey that builds capabilities over time.

Our research identified four levels of maturity or sophistication to categorize actions that can be taken. Most basic is digitizing and structuring the data, which is really the step before the use of big data. It consists of the steps that ensure the data are generated, structured, and organized in such a way that they can be used either directly by end users or for further analysis. These techniques include "scrubbing" the data to remove errors and ensure data quality, placing data into standard forms, and adding metadata that describe the data being collected. The second level of sophistication requires making the data available, e.g., through networks, which is aligned with the first of the five categories of big data levers discussed earlier. It can be a powerful driver of value in and of itself, and it can also be an important first step in integrating datasets to create more meaningful business insight. The third level of sophistication is applying basic analytics, which essentially covers a range of methodologies, such as basic data comparisons, and relatively standardized quantitative analyses, e.g., those that do not require customized analyses to be designed by people with deep analytical skills. The fourth and highest level is applying advanced analytics, such as the automated algorithms and real-time data analysis that often can create radical new business insight and models. They allow new levels of experimentation to develop optimal approaches to targeting customers and operations, and opening new big data opportunities with third parties. Leveraging big data at this level often requires the expertise of deep analytical talent.

In addition to examining the potential based on the level of capabilities within an organization, leaders can also examine different opportunities through the lens of the types of data identified during the data inventory. There is likely to be a set of opportunities related to capturing value from the proprietary datasets that an organization already has, particularly through additional analyses. For example, a health care provider might discover that it can analyze a set of clinical outcomes data to better identify the sources of medical errors. A second category of opportunities comes from adding new sets of data that can be captured or acquired (public and purchased) to these analyses. These datasets will often involve nonstandard data types, because these are data that are not usually used within the organization. For instance, an insurance company might discover that adding remote sensing data (images from satellites) can help it to better assess real-estate property risks. A third set of opportunities comes from considering new business and business models that are built fundamentally on big data, and not necessarily based on the same kinds of analyses that support existing businesses. For example, a payments provider might find that it create a new business by selling consumer insights based on the data streams it generates (so-called "exhaust data") while processing payments.

Organizations should also watch for the potential disruptions big data can underpin. Within the context of the big data value chain (Exhibit 39), aggregation and analysis are becoming increasingly valuable so data generators are adding those capabilities to more fully realize potential value as well as to defend against new entrants focusing solely on aggregation and analysis. For example, a big data retailer such as Tesco plays along the entire value chain to realize fullest potential. It taps its loyalty program to collect customer purchase data, which it then analyzes to inform a variety of decisions, including the micro-segmentation of its customers to optimize product mix, pricing, and promotions. Another example of forward integration in the data value chain is large health care payors, some of whom are getting into the business of aggregating and analyzing clinical data with claims data, to provide data services to customers such as pharmaceutical companies. Again, moving into aggregation and analysis may be a defensive move to preempt new entrants. In some sectors, third-party data aggregators, which do not generate data themselves, provide value-added service on top of the aggregated data to benefit customers. In financial services, for instance, the online company Mint (acquired by Intuit), aggregates financial information about individuals and provides value-added services (e.g., financial planning tools), even though it does not generate financial data itself. Mint and others using this business model may pose a threat to traditional financial institutions by owning customer relationships through their more comprehensive view of a consumer's entire financial position.

Organizations should also watch for the emergence of cross-sector domains, such as personal location data, where innovations are happening very quickly. They often have highly fragmented data value chains, with many stakeholders playing different roles, all trying to figure out business models that will maximize their share of the profit pool.

Indeed, the need for scale of data and IT infrastructure may become a critical driver toward consolidation, which can be both an opportunity and threat, in sectors where subscale players are abundant. The health care provider space is a good example where many relatively small physician practices remain. As they move into the digital age of electronic medical records and start trying to derive benefit from data, they may find it economical to merge with others to increase scale.

Increased data access, facilitated by the cloud, may also disrupt business and operation models. Many examples of distributed co-creation involve collaboration with external partners and customers to perform many corporate functions, from R&D (e.g., open source software development) to marketing (e.g., online advertising competition) and customer service (e.g., online customer support communities), that have traditionally been done internally by employees.

Exhibit 38

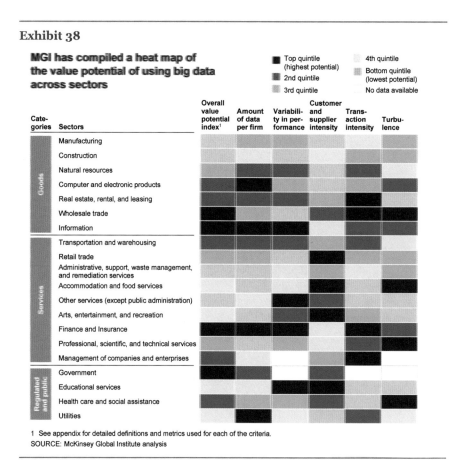

MGI has compiled a heat map of the value potential of using big data across sectors

Legend: ■ Top quintile (highest potential) | 4th quintile
■ 2nd quintile | ■ Bottom quintile (lowest potential)
3rd quintile | No data available

Categories	Sectors	Overall value potential index[1]	Amount of data per firm	Variability in performance	Customer and supplier intensity	Transaction intensity	Turbulence
Goods	Manufacturing						
	Construction						
	Natural resources						
	Computer and electronic products						
	Real estate, rental, and leasing						
	Wholesale trade						
	Information						
Services	Transportation and warehousing						
	Retail trade						
	Administrative, support, waste management, and remediation services						
	Accommodation and food services						
	Other services (except public administration)						
	Arts, entertainment, and recreation						
	Finance and Insurance						
	Professional, scientific, and technical services						
	Management of companies and enterprises						
Regulated and public	Government						
	Educational services						
	Health care and social assistance						
	Utilities						

1 See appendix for detailed definitions and metrics used for each of the criteria.
SOURCE: McKinsey Global Institute analysis

3. BUILD UP INTERNAL CAPABILITIES TO CREATE A DATA-DRIVEN ORGANIZATION

Organizations will need to have the right people and processes to capture value from the use of big data. On people, MGI research indicates that the key sets of talent that will be in increasingly short supply are deep analytical talent to execute big data analyses; managers and analysts who know how to request and consume big data analyses; and supporting technology personnel to implement big data. We focus on the first two categories in this section and address the third in the following section on implementing an enterprise data strategy.

Best practice big data companies have built sufficient scale in a core group of deep analytical talent, upon which the rest of their organization can draw. Given the potential competition for this talent, organizations must recruit deep analytical talent aggressively. This could include sourcing talent from other geographies or procuring some analytical services from vendors. One important point to note is that early hires are critical because they are the ones who build the teams. It is difficult to find people who are willing to hire their replacements, so hiring the most capable people early on is the best way to build a highly effective team. One financial services company respected for its use of data and experimentation, for instance, has identified a network of target institutions that are known for turning out superior deep analytical talent and that are in close proximity to headquarters. The company has developed a relationship with these institutions so it not only has a prominent presence during recruiting season, but also uses the institutions as ongoing training avenues, where the company sends deep analytical employees to get recharged and learn new techniques.

Leaders will also need to figure out how to organize this cadre of deep analytical talent so that as they form an internal community or center of excellence, they are effectively connected to the rest of the organization and can collaborate well with business leaders. Furthermore, retaining and motivating this valuable cadre of talent will, in a way similar to the case of other high-level knowledge workers, require monetary and, more importantly, intrinsic incentives such as interesting problems to solve.[94]

But having a core set of deep analytical talent is not enough to transform an organization, especially if the key business leaders and analysts do not know how to take advantage of this big data capability. All of the business leaders in an organization will have to develop a baseline understanding of analytical techniques in order to become effective users of these types of analyses. Organizations can modify their recruiting criteria to take this requirement into account, but more importantly, they will need to develop training programs to increase the capabilities of their current management and analyst ranks. A basic statistics program or a series of classes in data analysis at a local college or university, for instance, could create a team of highly motivated managers and analysts that could begin this transformation. Capital One, the financial services firm, has created an internal training institute, Capital One University, which offers a professional program on testing and experiment design, for instance. With the right capabilities in place, organizations must align incentives, structures, and workflows so that employees at all levels leverage insights derived from big data. The UK retailer Tesco, for example, has developed a strong data-driven mind-set from top leadership to the front line. It has integrated customer intelligence into its operations at all levels from a variety of consumer-targeted big data strategies. At Famous Footwear, the shoe retailer, the executive team meets with the testing head every two weeks to discuss results and plan data gathering and evaluation programs. At Amazon.com, it is said that Jeff Bezos fired a group of Web designers who changed the company Web site without conducting experiments to determine the effects on customer behavior. At all of these companies, big data and its most powerful levers are an integral part of management dialogues and the organization's culture.

4. DEVELOP ENTERPRISE INFORMATION STRATEGY TO IMPLEMENT TECHNOLOGY

To prepare for a big data world, organizations should develop an integrated data strategy for the entire enterprise. Data models, architectures, and attributes of solutions need to be considered holistically. Taking customer data as an example, a common problem is for discrete business units, in silos, to develop their own data strategies without planning to share or aggregate data across the organization. As a result, organizations often discover that they do not even have a common definition of their customers and attributes that apply across lines of business. Even within the same business unit, such differences can occur. The lack of a customer-centric view severely limits the organization's ability to use any of the powerful big data levers to create new value. An effective enterprise data strategy must include interoperable data models, transactional data architecture, integration architecture, analytical architecture, security and compliance, and frontline services.

Many organizations will require additional investment in IT hardware, software, and services to capture, store, organize, and analyze large datasets. The level

---

94 Peter F. Drucker, *Management challenges for the 21st century* (New York, NY: Harper Business, 1999).

of investment will vary considerably depending on a company's current state of IT capability and maturity. IT leaders will need to assess and identify any gaps in the technology their enterprise has available for effectively capturing, storing, aggregating, communicating, and analyzing data. They will have to work with the organization's business leaders to develop business cases for new investments and then prioritize that spending.

Despite the need for a comprehensive enterprise data strategy, it can often be helpful to begin implementation on very targeted projects in order to learn what works and to begin developing capabilities (see our recommendation about experimentation in the section "Identify potential value creation opportunities" above). For example, Kaiser Permanente in California initially concentrated on one IT project exclusively for patients with long-term conditions by creating specific disease registries and panel management solutions, rather than an all-encompassing IT solution that addresses a range of problems. This led to much faster time to impact.

5. ADDRESS DATA POLICY ISSUES

Addressing privacy and security issues will become paramount as more data increasingly travel across boundaries for various purposes. Privacy, in particular, not only requires attention to compliance with laws and regulations, but also is fundamental to an organization's trust relationships with its customers, business partners, employees, and other stakeholders. Certainly, organizations will need policies that comply with privacy laws and any government privacy regulations. But in developing a privacy policy, organizations will need to thoughtfully consider what kind of legal agreements, and, more importantly, trust expectations, it wants to establish with its stakeholders. And it will need to communicate its policies clearly to its stakeholders, especially customers, as they become increasingly savvy and concerned about what is known about them and how that information can potentially be used.

As part of the enterprise data strategy, organizations will need to clearly define and implement an enterprise risk strategy that includes all of their IT functions. This strategy must include a thorough risk assessment of the enterprise that assesses everything, from the likelihood of physical break-in, to the probability of hackers penetrating a mainframe, but perhaps most importantly, the risks of people with authorized access using that access for purposes that are counter to the organization's goals. There is a range of IT solutions (e.g., VPNs, intranet firewalls, threat monitoring) that can help to manage data privacy and security risks.

Organizational leaders will also have to wrestle with legal issues relating to their stance on intellectual property for data, how they will think about liability, etc. These are topics that clearly require specialized legal counsel, but with an approach that takes into account multiple considerations, including strategy, relationships with customers, partners and employees, and technology.

□ □ □

Competing and capturing value using big data will require leaders to address specific barriers across talent, technology, privacy and security, organizational culture, and incentives to access data. It is urgent that organization leaders start identifying or refining the role of big data in their business plans and start laying the enablers in place to realize value.

6. Implications for policy makers

The value potential underpinned by the use of big data will not be realized unless government and policy makers, in addition to leaders of individual organizations, understand and respond to the range of barriers and enablers we have identified. Our research has demonstrated that big data is not only a powerful engine of competition and growth for individual companies, but that, in aggregate, it also can move the needle on productivity, innovation, and competitiveness for entire sectors and economies in both the developed and developing worlds.

Forward-thinking policy makers will keep pace with the development of big data and find timely solutions to the barriers that today stand in the way of capturing its full value. Action may be required at both the national and international levels if policy makers are to help organizations make the most of the big data opportunity. Just as we are seeing early evidence of firms skilled at using big data pulling ahead of their competition, the use of big data could play a substantial role in country competitiveness.

Policy makers must consider the choices they should make in order to help individual firms in their economies capture value out of using big data. The major areas where policy can play a role are building human capital (e.g., improving the supply of graduates knowledgeable about big data and easing immigration restrictions); aligning incentives to ensure access to data; addressing privacy and security concerns; establishing intellectual property frameworks; overcoming technological barriers to data; and promoting information and communication technology infrastructure. Government policy makers in many economies are already addressing, or at least discussing, these areas. This is a task that they must start to address with some urgency. Without appropriate rules, laws, guidelines, and incentives, the economies that are less progressive in these areas will risk being at a competitive disadvantage to those that appreciate the dynamics and value potential of big data.

1. BUILD HUMAN CAPITAL FOR BIG DATA

Governments can act in a variety of ways to help increase the supply of talent necessary to leverage big data. First, governments can put in place education initiatives to increase the pipeline of graduates with the right skills. In the United States, for instance, there is a push at the federal, state, and local levels to support more science, technology, engineering, and mathematics (STEM) education. Most other OECD governments also recognize the need for more STEM graduates who are historically underrepresented in those fields, including women. However, the needs for deep analytical talent are more specific even than this—more graduates with advanced training in statistics and machine learning (a subdiscipline of computer science) will be necessary. A second way for governments to increase the supply of talent is to reduce barriers to accessing these pools in other regions, i.e., through remote work or the immigration of skilled workers.

The challenge of developing a large number of organizational leaders and analysts in business, government, and the social sectors who have basic understanding of analytical techniques is on a far larger scale. At a minimum, new knowledge workers already in the educational pipeline on their way into the workforce should be educated on these topics; a mandatory course in statistics/decision science, with a module on experimental design, should become part of the curriculum in fields such as business administration and other management disciplines. But waiting for a whole new generation of graduates will be insufficient. Government could create incentives to train existing managers and analysts in these techniques.

We also discovered in our research that detailed national workforce data about knowledge workers, by occupational category and industry, was difficult to find outside of the United States (including roles requiring deep analytical skills, as well as management and analyst roles, amongst others). Several countries could provide very detailed data about manufacturing-related occupations (e.g., "precious metal forging"), but had very broad categories for knowledge workers (e.g., "bankers"). Based on the principle that "you can't manage what you can't measure," policy makers in these countries could direct their labor statistics agencies to begin collecting more detailed data about employment in knowledge worker categories (ideally, in standard categories that would allow cross-country comparisons). This data would better inform their decisions about how to develop human capital, i.e., knowledge workers more generally, and for big data-related positions specifically.

2. ALIGN INCENTIVES TO PROMOTE DATA SHARING FOR THE GREATER GOOD

One of the most important enablers of value creation from big data is combining data from multiple sources. But in many cases markets for data have not yet been developed, or there are market failures for the sharing or trading of data. Governments can play an important role in creating the conditions for the functioning of effective markets, including setting rules related to intellectual property, the arbitration of disputes, and so on. For example, the requirement to create health information exchanges in the US health care sector is designed to ensure that sanitized clinical data can be shared across providers so that the system can fully utilize data on the comparative effectiveness of treatments.

Where there are market failures, such as a lack of self-interested incentives for a particular stakeholder group to make its data available, policy makers might have to apply the lever of regulation to ensure that data are shared. For example, there is tremendous reluctance to release data that expose errors (e.g., doctor or pilot mistakes) because of the reputational risk it poses for providers.[95] But government has a clear interest in making sure that these data are shared because doing so is one of the key enablers for reducing systemwide risks from such mistakes. Mandating the collection and release of such data might become necessary. For example, governments might require public companies to provide financial data in standardized electronic form. In the wake of the recent global financial crisis, many governments already take the view that considerable improvement in the transparency of financial reporting is necessary to mitigate systemic risks to the financial system.

---

95 For example, airline pilots might not necessarily like the fact that cockpit voice and data recorders can reveal errors they make while flying, but release of data from these devices to safety agencies after an accident is mandatory in order to improve the safety of the overall system.

In the public sector, where lack of competitive pressure limits efficiency and productivity, transparency can be a powerful tool. Openness and sharing of big data can be a critical lever and enabler of improved performance. Increasingly, policy makers require government agencies to intensify their measurement of activities and programs and then display that information in ways that are easily accessible to the public. This not only gives agencies tools for better management, but also it gives the public a way to hold the agencies accountable and gauge their performance in a quantifiable way. That public pressure can act as a significant incentive for agencies to improve performance, reduce costs, and boost productivity.

3. DEVELOP POLICIES THAT BALANCE THE INTERESTS OF COMPANIES WANTING TO CREATE VALUE FROM DATA AND CITIZENS WANTING TO PROTECT THEIR PRIVACY AND SECURITY

Although tremendous value, including consumer surplus, can be unlocked through the use of big data, the fact remains that many citizens are suspicious about the use of highly personal information. Citizens will continue to want their privacy rights clearly articulated, and businesses need to be able to know—and be able to anticipate any changes in—what data they can and cannot use. In some cases, markets for personal information could develop, but in other cases, traditional market mechanisms might not suffice to develop practices that protect privacy and security.

In the future, the effective design and enforcement of privacy laws will be critical not only for protecting customers, but also for providing assurance that the value of their consent to share data will far outweigh the potential risks. One challenge for policy makers will be to keep pace with big data developments, such as those involving fast-developing personal location data. Of course, governments, nonprofit organizations, and the private sector will need to develop education programs so the public can fully understand how much personal information is available, where and how it is used, and whether individuals are willing to allow this usage.

Most developed countries already have agencies that are responsible for creating and enforcing guidelines and laws concerning commercial and individual data privacy in general. In the United States, the Federal Trade Commission, for instance, uses its Fair Information Practice Principles as a guideline for dealing with security and privacy issues. Along the same lines, the OECD has issued guidelines on the Protection of Privacy and Transborder Flows of Personal Data, while the European Union has its Data Protection Directive. All of these guidelines and laws contain similar elements of reporting and protection. Germany has a federal commissioner who actively monitors industry for data protection compliance. South Korea's Data Protection Act is enforced by two separate government agencies.

In parallel, businesses and governments will almost certainly want strong laws prohibiting hacking and other security invasions to protect their own operations as much as possible, and they will want effective enforcement of those laws. Protecting critical IT infrastructure is important both to ensure that organizations can access and use data securely, and to safeguard national security, as cyber attacks become increasingly sophisticated and bold. For instance, cyber attacks against portions of a country's financial infrastructure (e.g., credit card processing facilities) can result in the release of sensitive personal information about millions of individuals and loss of trust in electronic markets.

4. ESTABLISH EFFECTIVE INTELLECTUAL PROPERTY FRAMEWORKS TO ENSURE INNOVATION

We will undoubtedly continue to see many innovations emerging along the data value chain in the age of big data. Innovative technology to better generate and capture data will emerge. Advances in storage and analytics will continue as organizations increasingly need to store ever greater amount of data, access and analyze them, sometimes in near real time. These innovations require an effective intellectual property system, which will both ensure incentives for creating valuable data and enable the effective sharing and integration of different pools of data. There will be increasing demand for more effective and efficient means of establishing intellectual property rights (e.g., copyright and patents) and adjudicating disputes.

5. ADDRESS TECHNOLOGY BARRIERS AND ACCELERATE R&D IN TARGETED AREAS

Policy makers can play a role in helping to overcome technology issues related to the use of big data, from facilitating the development of standards and guidelines regarding IT tools or data pools, to encouraging R&D in critical areas where gaps exist today.

Standards covering IT tools or certain types of data are critical so that data can be shared to create the necessary scale to enable the kind of analytics that create value. These standards can emerge from industry standard-setting bodies, but government can play an enabling role. For example, in the US health care arena, the Standards and Certification Criteria for Electronic Health Records (EHR) to be issued by the Office of the National Coordinator for Health Information Technology will identify the standards necessary for certification of EHR technologies so that medical professionals and hospitals are assured that the system they adopt can perform as required.

Policy makers can also accelerate big data research. Government can directly sponsor basic research. For example, the U.S. National Science Foundation funds programs in both computer science and mathematics, while the EU has put in place the Research Framework Programme, designed to be the main instrument for coordinating and allocating research funding in science and technology areas in Europe.

Governments can also consider how to deploy incentives, e.g., tax expenditures or other financial support, to help overcome technological barriers to leveraging big data. Sometimes, there is a mismatch between who must make a technology investment and who will receive the benefits of that investment. For instance, in US health care, providers are the primary investors in electronic medical record technology, but the benefits felt in the form of optimized health care go disproportionately to payors and patients. The American Recovery and Reinvestment Act of 2009 provided some $20 billion to health providers and their support sectors to invest in electronic record systems and health information exchanges to create the scale of clinical data needed for many of the health care big data levers to work.

6. ENSURE INVESTMENTS IN UNDERLYING INFORMATION AND COMMUNICATION TECHNOLOGY INFRASTRUCTURE

For organizations to leverage large datasets, basic infrastructure needs to be in place from electricity grids that power information technology to communication networks that enable data to travel. Judging from the approaches we observe in different countries, the spectrum of possible policy interventions to encourage infrastructure to be built and maintained can vary significantly.

Many countries have created specific incentives and initiatives targeted at expanding infrastructure. For example, the US government has put in place a number of monetary incentives to encourage the build-out of broadband infrastructure (e.g., rural broadband project) and the implementation of electronic medical records. The US government has also proposed a far-reaching national wireless development program that involves a voluntary incentive auction to free up spectrum as well as wireless spectrum reallocation, with the goal of covering 98 percent of the country with 4G high-speed accessibility. Other governments also are taking action to foster competition in infrastructure markets to drive down costs to end customers and to broaden access. South Korea, for instance, is providing subsidies for broadband subscription by certain groups (e.g., low income) but, like Japan and some European countries, explicitly requires broadband providers that own the network to share the facilities at a fee.

In the years ahead, policy makers should make infrastructure an explicit part of their approach to big data.

☐ ☐ ☐

Policy makers can play a vital enabling role to ensure that organizations make the most of the potential of big data in the key areas of talent, R&D, and infrastructure, as well as to foster innovation in this dynamic arena. Some of the policy action that they can, and should, take will involve practical nuts-and-bolts moves that take effort but are not controversial. The more complex task will be ensuring that legislation strike the right balance between freeing organizations to use data to the significant extent they need in order to capture its full potential, and assuaging fears among the public about compromising privacy and personal security. This is a balance that requires thoughtful consideration and one that policy makers should not shy away from addressing.

Appendix

Construction of indices on value potential and ease of capture

From our analysis of big data in five domains, we reached a sense of what characteristics indicate higher or lower value potential from the use of big data to capture value from its use, as well as higher or lower barriers in realizing that value in different sectors. Using these insights, we created two indices: (1) an index on value potential, and (2) an index on the ease of capture. Each of these indices comprises multiple criteria which give us a relative sense of which sectors may be poised for greater gains and which sectors would face the toughest barriers. We do not claim that these indices give a full picture, but we believe that they give a good sense of both the potential value available and the ease or otherwise of its capture across sectors.

VALUE POTENTIAL INDEX

The five criteria we use in this index act as a proxy for how well a sector can benefit from one of the five transformative opportunities we have discussed in this report (Exhibit A1):

1. **Amount of data per firm.** The larger the amount of data per firm, the more it indicates that a firm is likely to be able to benefit from increasing transparency in terms of data. We used the storage available per firm as a proxy. We built upon our data mapping analysis to estimate the available data storage, in bytes, in 2009 in each sector in the United States. We then divided that by the number of firms with more than 1,000 employees (to avoid skewing the numbers by the large number of small businesses and individual proprietors).

2. **Variability in performance.** The higher the variability, the more it indicates a firm can benefit from the use of data and experimentation to expose variability and improve performance. We used the variability in EBITDA (earnings before interest tax depreciation and amortization) as a proxy. Within each sector, we took the EBITDA of major companies (with greater than $500 million in sales) from 2002 to 2007 and identified the 10th and 90th percentile EBITDA. The difference between the top and bottom performers became the variability we measured.

3. **Customer and supplier intensity.** The more customers and suppliers a firm has, the greater its potential to apply segmentation to tailor courses of action. We used the number of frontline employees (defined as those who interface with customers or suppliers) per firm as a proxy. We used data from the US Bureau of Labor Statistics to identify the number of frontline employees (major occupations include Standard Occupation Classification codes 41 such as sales clerks and agents, and 43 such as administrative workers) in the latest year available. We then divided by the number of firms with more than 1,000 employees

4. **Transaction intensity.** The higher the transaction intensity, the more likely the sector can benefit from the use of automated algorithms to augment or replace

human decision making. We used the amount of processing power of an average firm in a sector as a proxy. To arrive at a relative sense of processing power, we used capital stock data for PCs and mainframes by sector from the US Bureau of Economic Analysis and divided by the number of firms with more than 1,000 employees in each sector.

5. **Turbulence.** Turbulence, or how frequently leaders and laggards in a sector change place, is a proxy for the amount of innovative disruptions to which a sector is susceptible. We hypothesize that the higher the turbulence, the greater the likelihood that a sector will benefit from the use of big data to innovate business models, products, and services. Within each sector, we calculated the turnover percentage—the number of new companies placed in the top 20 ranking in 2011 compared with 2006, divided by 20.

Once we quantified each criterion (the proxy), we gave each sector a score of from one to five based on the quintile into which it falls into for each criterion. The overall value potential index is the average of the scores across the five criteria.

Exhibit A1

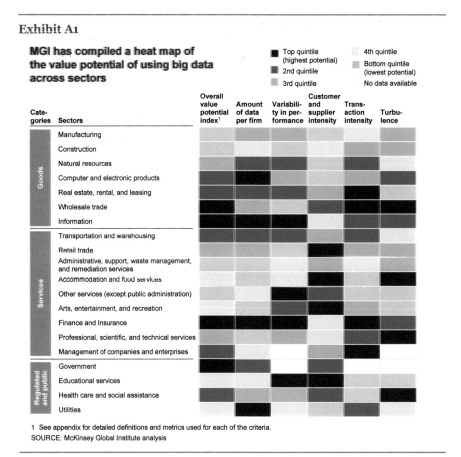

MGI has compiled a heat map of the value potential of using big data across sectors

Legend: ■ Top quintile (highest potential) ■ 2nd quintile ▪ 3rd quintile · 4th quintile ▪ Bottom quintile (lowest potential) · No data available

Categories	Sectors	Overall value potential index[1]	Amount of data per firm	Variability in performance	Customer and supplier intensity	Transaction intensity	Turbulence
Goods	Manufacturing						
	Construction						
	Natural resources						
	Computer and electronic products						
	Real estate, rental, and leasing						
	Wholesale trade						
	Information						
Services	Transportation and warehousing						
	Retail trade						
	Administrative, support, waste management, and remediation services						
	Accommodation and food services						
	Other services (except public administration)						
	Arts, entertainment, and recreation						
	Finance and Insurance						
	Professional, scientific, and technical services						
	Management of companies and enterprises						
Regulated and public	Government						
	Educational services						
	Health care and social assistance						
	Utilities						

1 See appendix for detailed definitions and metrics used for each of the criteria.
SOURCE: McKinsey Global Institute analysis

EASE OF CAPTURE INDEX

This index is made up of four criteria, each of which aligns with a key barrier to the use of big data that we have identified (Exhibit A2):

1. **Talent.** The more deep analytical talent a firm has, the better a position it is in to realize value from big data. We divided the number of deep analytical talent in 2008 by the number of firms with more than 1,000 employees in each sector.

2. **IT intensity.** The more IT assets a sector has on average, the lower the technology barriers to be overcome. We calculated IT stock using data from the US Bureau of Economic Analysis and divided that total by the number of firms with more than 1,000 employees in each sector.

3. **Data-driven mind-set.** This indicates how receptive the organization is to using big data to create value. We leveraged the latest survey results conducted on IT strategy by McKinsey's Business Technology Office, which asked leaders the degree to which their organizations make decisions based on experience and opinions or based on data.

4. **Data availability.** We use the relative number of databases related to each sector in a proprietary corpus of data as a proxy for how accessible data is in a sector.

Again, once we quantified each criterion (the proxy), we gave each sector a score of one to five based on the quintile into which it falls for each criterion. The overall ease of capture index is the average of the scores across the four criteria.

Exhibit A2

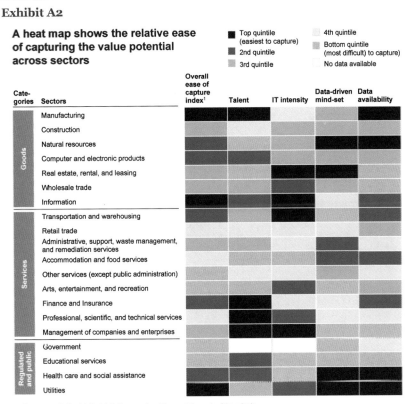

A heat map shows the relative ease of capturing the value potential across sectors

1 See appendix for detailed definitions and metrics used for each of the criteria.
SOURCE: McKinsey Global Institute analysis

Data map methodology

Several research groups have studied the amount of data that enterprises and individuals are generating, storing, and consuming in studies that have used various definitions and scopes (Exhibit A3). However, there are no insights available thus far about the variations among sectors. For this reason, we undertook a brief modeling exercise to estimate the amount of data generated and stored in different sectors, both on an aggregate basis and on a per firm basis.

To estimate the amount of data generated and stored in aggregate, our model relies on four key inputs and assumptions:

1. **Annual storage capacities shipped by sector.** We used industry reports from IDC and Gartner that provide the total number of bytes shipped each year in external disks, including storage area networks (SAN), network attached storage (NAS), and direct attached storage (DAS). These data are available by sector and by selected geographies.

2. **Average replacement cycle of storage.** We used a McKinsey estimate for the average replacement cycle of storage. This allowed us to estimate the total available (cumulative) storage in a given year.

3. **Utilization rate.** We used a McKinsey estimate of the average percentage of storage utilized at a given point. This allowed us to estimate the amount of incremental data capacity used (also referred to as "new data stored" in our report) in a given year.

4. **Duplication rate.** For security and other reasons, every piece of data is often stored multiple times (e.g., for backup, recorded in different systems for a variety of uses). McKinsey specialists provided us with an average estimate that allowed us to estimate the amount of "unique" data generated and stored in a given year.

We applied a similar approach to estimating the amount of data generated and stored by consumers. In this case, we included key devices that store content genuinely generated by users, namely solid-state disk and hard disk drives in PCs, notebooks, and certain electronics. We did not include consumer devices and storage components such as DVDs, CDs, and digital video recorders that predominantly contain content that users have not generated (e.g., generated by media companies).

Our estimates are in line with results from previous research. Our estimate of 7.4 exabytes of new data stored is most comparable to the 25 exabytes of data storage capacity estimated by Hilbert and López for server and mainframe hard disks.

We extended our analysis to a per firm level in the United States, where data on the number for firms are most readily available. We took the estimated available storage capacities, as well as new data stored, for different sectors in the United States, and divided by the number of firms (with more than 1,000 employees) in the corresponding sectors. Data on the number of firms came from the US Bureau of Labor Statistics and Dun & Bradstreet. We chose to include only firms of at least medium size—i.e., those with more than 1,000 employees.

Exhibit A3

How MGI's estimate of the size of big data compares with previous external estimates

	What was measured	Amount of data	Year of estimate
MGI storage-based approach	• New data stored in enterprise external disk storage in a year • New data stored by consumers in a year	• 7.4×10^{18} bytes (includes replicas) • 6.8×10^{18} bytes	• For 2010
IDC/EMC[1] Digital Universe	• Annual digital data captured (includes all generated, stored or not) • Includes more than 60 types of devices • Did not include information consumption by users through TV, video gaming[1]	• ~800×10^{18} bytes	• For 2009
UCSD	• Includes both digital and analog data for TV, radio, phone, print, computer, comp. games, movies, recorded music, etc. • Measured data from consumption perspective[2]	• 3.6×10^{21} bytes (total consumption US only)	• For 2008

Hilbert, López	• Capacities for specific technologies
	  — Server and mainframe hard disks
	  — Other hard disks
	  — Digital tape
	  — PC hard disk
	• Total digital storage capacity
		
		• 24.5×10^{18} bytes
		• 6.49×10^{18} bytes
		• 32.5×10^{18} bytes
		• 123×10^{18} bytes
		• 276×10^{18} bytes
			• For 2007

1 Includes chip cards, floppy disks, camera, video games, mobiles, memory cards, media players, CDs, DVDs, Blue Ray disks, PC and server hard disks.
2 Consumption is defined as the data each time used by the user.
SOURCE: IDC white papers on Digital Universe, sponsored by EMC; Bohn and Short, *How Much Information? 2009: Report on American Consumers*, January 2010; Hilbert and López, "The world's technological capacity to store, communicate, and compute information," *Science*, February 2011; McKinsey Global Institute analysis

Estimating value potential in health care (United States)

In our analysis of big data in US health care, we focused on levers or initiatives where large datasets are a necessary precondition for creating value—but are often not sufficient by themselves to generate any value. We concede that, in most cases, the realization of value requires significant structural changes including legislative adjustments, new incentives, and reimbursement schemes, as well as overcoming barriers such as privacy concerns.

We define long-term potential as value that can be captured in a ten-year period in a scenario that assumes sufficient structural changes are made. Some of the levers may overlap with other health care information technology initiatives and proposed health care reforms although we explicitly excluded value accruing from the pure implementation of IT. For example, we did not include the time doctors and nurses save from using electronic medical records and therefore being able to avoid handwriting charts and storing and retrieving charts on paper. At the same time, we included savings from reducing overtreatment (and undertreatment) in cases where analysis of clinical data contained in electronic medical records was able to determine optimal medical care.

To estimate the value potential of each of the big-data-enabled levers that we have identified, we used a tailored approach based on key drivers. These drivers typically include (1) base numbers, such as the number of hospitals, patients, clinical trials, or cost per base number for which we tended to use the latest year figure available; and (2) the breakdown of impact between, for instance, cost reduction, and increase in time to market. In estimating the potential impact of big data, we used US and international case studies with reported impact numbers wherever possible. In the remaining few cases, we relied on expert interviews. We know that several factors need to come together to generate value; nevertheless, we have assigned the full value of the identified levers to big data because it is not possible to break down

128

impact among contributing factors. We did, however, select case studies or expert estimates, on which we base the impact numbers, in a way that minimize any double counting of impact across the big data levers.

We scaled impact numbers from individual case studies appropriately to ascertain the impact on a sector or system-wide level and then on national health care expenditure. We assumed some fundamental complementary transformations such as nationwide adoption rates of enabling technologies (e.g., about 90 percent adoption of hospital electronic medical records) and structural changes (e.g., potential provider consolidation or formation of accountable care organizations). Although our estimates of the potential value released by big data assume some fundamental complementary changes, our estimates remain within the range of estimates made by researchers in academia, think tanks, and government (Exhibit A4).

To calculate the impact of big-data-enabled levers on productivity, we assumed that the majority of the quantifiable impact would be on reducing inputs. We held outputs constant—i.e., assuming the same level of health care quality. We know that this assumption will underestimate the impact as many of our big-data-enabled levers are likely to improve the quality of health by, for instance, ensuring that new drugs come to the market faster and patients receive optimal treatment.

Focusing on quantifying the productivity impact from efficiency savings, we then added the total potential across levers, excluding those where savings may not have any impact on overall national health care spending. We then projected those total savings forward and divided that total by future projected health care spending. The annualized rate is our estimate of the productivity impact of big data in health care.

Exhibit A4

CER and CDS were identified as key levers and can be valued based on different implementations and timelines
Estimated annual lever impact, $ billion

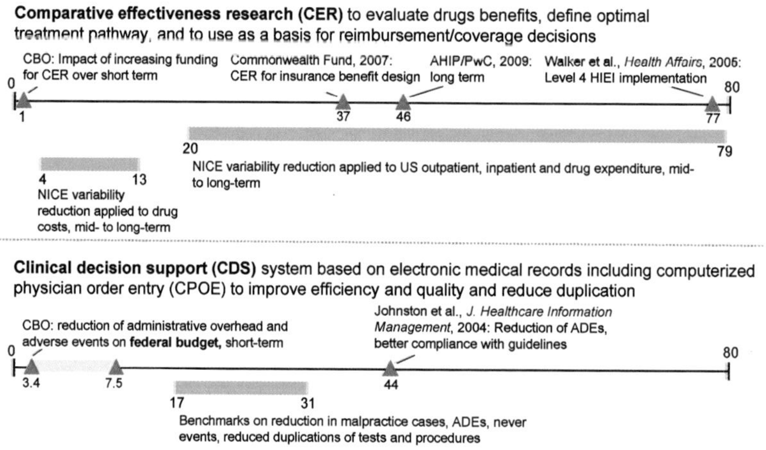

Comparative effectiveness research (CER) to evaluate drugs benefits, define optimal treatment pathway, and to use as a basis for reimbursement/coverage decisions

CBO: Impact of increasing funding for CER over short term — 1
Commonwealth Fund, 2007: CER for insurance benefit design — 37
AHIP/PwC, 2009: long term — 46
Walker et al., Health Affairs, 2005: Level 4 HIEI implementation — 77
0 ... 80

20 ... 79
NICE variability reduction applied to US outpatient, inpatient and drug expenditure, mid- to long-term

4 ... 13
NICE variability reduction applied to drug costs, mid- to long-term

Clinical decision support (CDS) system based on electronic medical records including computerized physician order entry (CPOE) to improve efficiency and quality and reduce duplication

CBO: reduction of administrative overhead and adverse events on **federal budget**, short-term
Johnston et al., J. Healthcare Information Management, 2004: Reduction of ADEs, better compliance with guidelines
0 ... 80
3.4 ... 7.5 ... 44

17 ... 31
Benchmarks on reduction in malpractice cases, ADEs, never events, reduced duplications of tests and procedures

SOURCE: Congressional Budget Office; PwC Health Industries; Walker et al., "The value of health care information exchange and interoperability," Health Affairs, 2005; Johnston, Pan, and Walker, "The value of CPOE in ambulatory settings," Journal of Healthcare Information Management, 2004

Estimating value potential in public sector administration (European Union)

To size the value potential of big data levers in European public sector administration, we drew on government operational and budget data (at aggregate and at department levels) and McKinsey's internal public sector expertise and took a micro-to-macro approach in our analysis.

First, we identified big data levers and quantified their potential to create value by focusing on two specific agencies—tax and labor—that are prototypical examples of administrative functions. We estimated the potential impact by drawing on best practices found around the world. Next we extrapolated the impact of the identified levers to a country's entire government by identifying other addressable subdepartments, and applying the potential improvement found in our agency-level analysis to the addressable portion, adjusted by relevance. Finally, we scaled up our estimates at the country level to all OECD economies in Europe.

We found three categories of benefits from the use of big data in public sector administration:

1. **Operational efficiency savings.** We applied the percentage of potential operational cost savings to estimated addressable European OECD government expenditure (net of transfers).

2. **Reduction of cost of fraud and errors.** We applied the percentage of potential fraud reduction to estimated addressable European OECD government transfer payments by multiplying the percentage of transfer payments. The estimated addressable transfer payment took into account the percentage of transfer payment that has a non-negligible amount of fraud and error and the estimated percentage of the cost of fraud and errors.

3. **Increase in tax revenue collection.** We applied a percentage potential reduction in the tax gap to the estimated European OECD government tax gap.

For the purposes of our analysis, we used the latest year of consistent government spending and taxation revenue data from the OECD.

We then translated monetary potential into productivity estimates. We define productivity as the amount of output produced in relation to the level of inputs required to produce that output. Improved productivity comes from both reducing inputs (given a fixed level of output) and increasing the quality or quantity of output (given a fixed level of input).

The productivity of the public sector is difficult to measure for two main reasons. First, many sectors don't have quantifiable output (e.g., national security). Second, even in sectors where outputs are evident, measurement is of limited usefulness without an assessment of whether those outputs add value to citizens and how that value changes over time.

From 1969 to 1994, the US Bureau of Labor Statistics experimented with productivity measures for key government functions but discontinued this effort because of budget cutbacks. In the United Kingdom, the Office of National Statistics responded to the Atkinson review in 2003 by establishing a Center for the Measurement of

Government Activity that has begun to produce a productivity index for some parts of government.

In the absence of established methodologies for measuring public sector productivity, we approximated quality-adjusted outputs using tax revenue and total inputs using total budget/spend. In our model, tax revenue was the only improved outcome, and we assumed that other outcomes such as the number of people put back to work were not affected.

In our methodology, annual productivity growth is the sum of annualized percentage increase in tax revenue and the annualized percentage decrease in total government budget. While this is a rough methodology, we believe that our estimates are reasonable as they are within the same range of other comparable estimates (Exhibit A5).

Exhibit A5

Productivity estimates: Public sector administration

Annual productivity growth
%

"Micro to macro" analyses from deep dive	Tax agency	0.7
	Labor agency	0.3
	Public sector administration	0.5
Comparisons with other data points	US public sector efficiency potential[1]	0.5 — 0.9 — 1.4
	Adoption of IT/online services at Job Centre Plus[2]	1.2
	IT contribution in private sector[3]	1.7

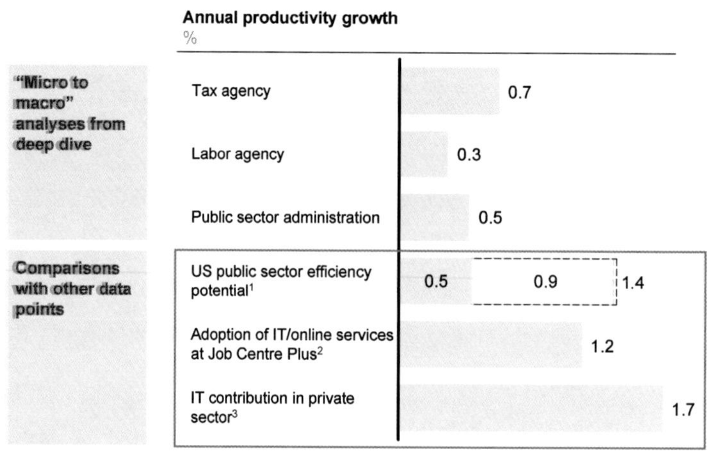

1 Dohrmann and Mendoca, "Boosting government productivity," *McKinsey Quarterly*.
2 P. Dunleavy, *Innovating Out of a Recession*, seminar, London School of Economics, London, June 2009.
3 Oliner and Sichel "Information Technology and Productivity: Where Are We Now and Where Are We Going," *Federal Reserve Bank of Atlanta Economic Review*, 2002
SOURCE: McKinsey Global Institute analysis

Estimating value potential in retail (United States)

To arrive at estimates of the value created by big data for retail firms, which we then extended to estimate a total value estimate for the whole sector, we used a combination of client case studies, academic and industry research, and interviews with experts.

Starting with our estimate of the potential value created at the level of individual firms, we used a model that depends on four key drivers (Exhibit A6).

1. Subsector cost structure archetypes, which gives us the various cost buckets as a percentage of sales. We used US Census Bureau data and McKinsey analysis.

2. Estimates of impact by individual levers, expressed as a percentage reduction on a cost bucket or percentage increase in volume or price (Exhibit A7). We used extensive interviews with McKinsey experts drawing on their client experience, as well as published case studies.

Exhibit A6

Retail: Diagram of model showing the impact of levers

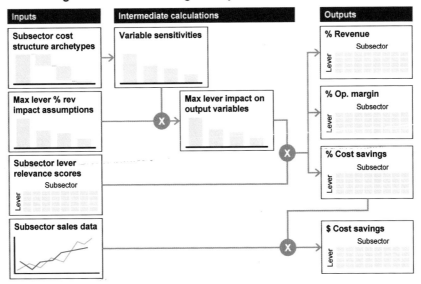

SOURCE: McKinsey Global Institute analysis

Exhibit A7

The impact of levers on labor productivity

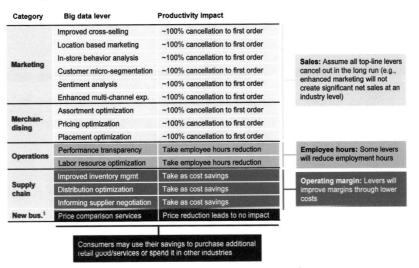

1 Impact of Web-based markets is difficult to quantify and we have excluded this from our calculations.
SOURCE: McKinsey Global Institute analysis

3. Subsector level lever relevance heat map that tells us the relative relevance of a lever in a particular subsector. Levers have different potential for different subsectors either because they have different degrees of relevance or because subsectors will already be operating with varying degrees of big data maturity.

4. Subsector sales that allow us to calculate not just the percentage impact on margins but in absolute dollars. We used a combination of estimates from the US Bureau of Economic Analysis, US Census Bureau, and Moody's.

Our firm-level analysis tells us the potential impact of an individual retailer that adopts the big data levers, relative to competitors that do not.

To extend our firm-level analysis to the sector-wide level, we calculated potential productivity gains conservatively using those levers specific to operations and supply chains, for instance, that reduce costs. This is because we believe that any nominal sales increase gained by individual firms are unlikely to accrue to gains in total nominal sales across the whole of the retail sector, given that consumers' total retail spending is primarily influenced by overall economic growth. We agree that this means that our estimate is likely to be conservative. Nevertheless, our estimates of a 1 to 2 percent productivity gain assuming all efficiency levers are pulled and a 0.5 to 1 percent excluding the impact of the sourcing lever (which assumes no net effect when suppliers are also pulling the same lever) are comparable to the range of IT impacts on the productivity of nonfarm sectors in general (Exhibit A8).

Exhibit A8

Following this approach leads to significant labor productivity compound annual growth rates from the implementation of big data levers

Big data labor productivity improvements in the US retail industry over next 10 years
Compound annual growth rate, %

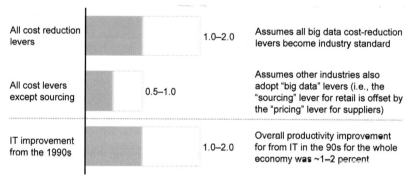

All cost reduction levers	1.0–2.0	Assumes all big data cost-reduction levers become industry standard
All cost levers except sourcing	0.5–1.0	Assumes other industries also adopt "big data" levers (i.e., the "sourcing" lever for retail is offset by the "pricing" lever for suppliers)
IT improvement from the 1990s	1.0–2.0	Overall productivity improvement for from IT in the 90s for the whole economy was ~1–2 percent

SOURCE: Jorgensen, Dale, Ho, and Stiroh, "A retrospective look at the US productivity growth resurgence," *Journal of Economic Perspectives*, 2008; McKinsey Global Institute analysis

Estimating value potential in personal location data (global)

For this case study, we drew on McKinsey's macroeconomic and industry expertise, external academic research, and market forecasts, as well as extensive findings in the available literature. By looking at the value chain of location-based applications, we examined both the amount of data generation and the potential to create value.

We estimated the amount of personal location data generated in each category of application or source device and in different geographic regions using the installed base of devices, usage behavior, and the frequency with which data are generated. To assess the potential value that data can generate, we scrutinized the major applications of personal location data and estimated the economic value of each application to end users—individual consumers, enterprises, and government organizations. While we have sized each of the identified applications or levers, we know that our total value potential estimate will be conservative, given new applications or levers will emerge in the future that we cannot predict today.

The underlying model and inputs used to measure economic value varied for each application. Take personal navigation applications as an illustration of our approach. We measured potential economic value through the metrics of time saved and reduced fuel consumption due to the use of classical navigation and "smart" traffic-enabled navigation. Inputs included the outcome of experiments in Western European cities, extrapolated globally based on rates of GPS adoption, driving behavior, and a congestion index calculated using the density of population and vehicles on available road infrastructure across all regions (Exhibit A9).

Exhibit A9

We have introduced a regional congestion index based on city/area population density and vehicle density

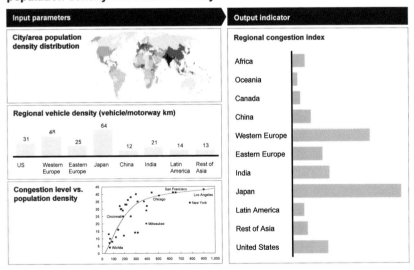

SOURCE: Eurostat; US Census; www.world-gazetteer.com; World Bank; McKinsey Global Institute analysis

Methodology for analyzing the supply and demand of analytical talent

We focused primarily on analyzing the supply and demand projections of analytical talent in the United States because of the availability of labor and education data at a granular level. We did analyze the supply situation globally in selected geographies where education data are readily available. In this appendix, we will first explain the US analysis and then the global analysis.

US analysis

First, we analyzed the supply and demand gap for three types of big data talent in 2018:

1. Deep analytical talent—people with the advanced training in statistics and machine learning who can analyze large volumes of data to derive business insights.

2. Data-savvy managers and analysts who have the skills to be effective consumers of big data insights—i.e., to pose the right questions for analysis, interpret and challenge the results, and take appropriate decisions.

3. Supporting technology personnel who develop, implement, and maintain the hardware and software tools needed to make use of big data including databases and analytic programs (Exhibit A10).

Exhibit A10

Big data talent is grouped into deep analytical, big data savvy, and supporting technology

	Deep analytical	Big data savvy	Supporting technology
Definitions	People who have advanced training in statistics and/or machine learning and conduct data analysis	People who have basic knowledge of statistics and/or machine learning and define key questions data can answer	People who service as database administrators and programmers
Occupations[1]	▪ Actuaries ▪ Mathematicians ▪ Operations research analysts ▪ Statisticians ▪ Mathematical technicians ▪ Mathematical scientists ▪ Industrial engineers ▪ Epidemiologist ▪ Economists	▪ Business and functional managers ▪ Budget, credit and financial analysts ▪ Engineers ▪ Life scientists ▪ Market research analysts ▪ Survey researchers ▪ Industrial-organizational psychologists ▪ Sociologist	▪ Computer and information scientists ▪ Computer programmers ▪ Computer software engineers for applications ▪ Computer software engineers for system software ▪ Computer system analysts ▪ Database administrators

These occupations comprise 51 occupations in the SOC across 170 industries as defined by the North American Industry Classification System (NAICS)

1 Occupations are defined by the Standard Occupational Code (SOC) of the US Bureau of Labor Statistics and used as the proxy for types of talent in labor force.
SOURCE: US Bureau of Labor Statistics; McKinsey Global Institute analysis

In the following, we will describe our methodology to project the supply and demand for deep analytical talent, though we also applied a similar methodology to the other two categories. We estimated supply and demand for deep analytical talent separately. In both estimates, however, employment data from 2008, the latest year for which complete data were available for analysis, serve as the base. We assume that the labor market cleared in 2008 (i.e., 2008 employment data represent both the supply and demand of labor).

We define people who have deep analytical talent as those with advanced training in statistics and/or machine learning. To estimate the 2008 base of this class of talent, we used US Bureau of Labor Statistics 2008 occupational employment data, making the assumption that occupation is an adequate representation of talent. Using the Standard Occupational Classification (SOC) system (SOC code is in parentheses), the occupations that we chose to represent deep analytical talent were actuaries (15-2011), mathematicians (15-2021), operational research analysts (15-2031), statisticians (15-2041), mathematical technicians (15-2091), mathematical scientists all other (15-2099), industrial engineers (17-2112), epidemiologists (19-1041), and economists (19-3011). For each of these occupational categories, we estimated the percentage of people that would have the requisite deep analytical skills.

We estimated the supply of deep analytical talent in 2018 using the 2008 base plus university graduates with relevant skills, plus immigration, minus attrition. We define the skills that are relevant to deep analytical talent among graduates to be majors and degrees that are consistent with SOC occupations. Using detailed statistics about US university graduates, we chose estimated ratios of graduates with bachelor's and master's degrees and doctorates in the following majors that have the relevant deep analytical skills: computer and information sciences, mathematics and statistics, engineering, physical sciences and science technology, biological and biomedical sciences, social sciences, and business.

We used two separate approaches to estimate the demand for deep analytical talent in 2018. The results of these two approaches are consistent. We based our first and more detailed approach on the current model used by the BLS. Demand for deep analytical talent in 2018 is driven by the growth of industries that employ these people and the share of this talent employed by these industries, estimated by the percentage of each occupation within a sector that are serving in a deep analytical capacity.

To simplify our model, we define industries using the North American Industry Classification System and group them into low, medium, and high data intensity according to their data storage capital stock per firm with 1,000 or more employees. We take this approach because we assume that industry demand for deep analytical talent will differ significantly according to how much data an industry generates and stores. For example, finance, a high-data-intensity sector, is likely to have more growth in demand for deep analytical talent.

In a world in which all big data levers are actively deployed by organizations across the economy, our first model assumes that all sectors will increase their demand for deep analytical talent at the fastest rate projected by BLS through 2018 in their respective group of industries according to data intensity. For example, in the high-data-intensity group, Internet services are projected to have the highest growth of deep analytical talent through 2018; thus we model other sectors in the high-data-intensity group to experience the same rate of growth as that of Internet services.

The second model we used is a firm-based demand model, which assumes that demand for deep analytical talent is driven differentially according to three main industry groups: financial and insurance industries (FIG); online (Internet service providers, Web search portals, data processing and housing services); and all other industries. This assumption reflects our interviews with industry leaders that suggested that FIG and online industries will require significantly more deep analytical talent per firm than those in other industries. We estimate the number of people with these skills needed in each industry group based on the number of firms in each employment size class and the expected number of deep analytical talent required per firm (differs by employment size class). The numbers of firms by industry are estimated using the Statistics of US Business (SUSB), the US Census, and Dun & Bradstreet.

Global analysis

We estimated the number of graduates with deep analytical talent in the United States internationally training in other countries using Euromonitor data on graduates by major by degree as well as data from local statistics offices where Euromonitor data are not available. We apply the ratios of US graduates to maintain consistency with the US estimate.

Key data sources

Data description	Data sources
Occupational employment	US Bureau of Labor Statistics (BLS)
Occupational employment projection	US Bureau of Labor Statistics (BLS)
Numbers of public and private firms by employment size	Statistics of US Businesses (SUSB)
Numbers of public firms with 1K+ employees by industry	Dun & Bradstreet (D&B)
Net capital stock by type	US Bureau of Economic Analysis (BEA)
Numbers of university graduates in the United States	National Center for Education Statistics, IPEDS Data Center
Numbers of university graduates globally	Euromonitor

Bibliography

Abele, Eberhard, Tobias Meyer, Ulrich Näher, Gernot Strube, and Richard Sykes, eds., *Global production: A handbook for strategy and implementation* (Berlin: Springer, 2008).

ABI research, *Consumer technology barometer: Mobile*, 2010.

Agrawal, R., T. Imielinski, and A. Swami, "Mining association rules between sets of items in large databases," SIGMOD Conference 1993: 207–216.

Akella, Janaki, Timo Kubach, Markus Löffler, and Uwe Schmid, *Data-driven management: Bringing more science into management*, McKinsey Technology Initiative Perspective, 2008.

America's Health Insurance Plans, *Technical Memo: Estimates of the potential reduction in health care costs from AHIP's affordability proposals*, June 2008.

Ayes, Ian, *Super crunchers: Why thinking-by-numbers is the new way to be smart* (New York: Bantam Books, 2007).

Baily, Martin N., Karen Croxson, Thomas Dohrmann, and Lenny Mendonca, *The public sector productivity imperative*, McKinsey & Company, March 2011.

Baker, Stephen, *The numerati* (New York: Houghton Mifflin, 2008).

Barber, Michael, Alastair Levy, and Lenny Mendoca, *Global trends affecting the public sector*, McKinsey white paper, February 2008.

Baumgarten, Jason, and Michael Chui, "E-government 2.0," *McKinsey Quarterly*, July 2009.

Benham, Lee, "The effect of advertising on the price of eyeglasses," *Journal of Law and Economics* 15(2), October 1972: 337–352.

Besley, Timothy, and Maitreesh Ghatak, "Status incentives," *American Economic Review* 98(2), 2008: 206–211.

Bohn, Roger, and James Short, *How much information? 2009: Report on American consumers*, University of California, San Diego, Global Information Industry Center, January 2010.

Bohn, Roger, James Short, and Chaitanya Baru, *How much information? 2010: Report on enterprise server information*, University of California, San Diego, Global Information Industry Center, January 2011.

Bollier, David, *The promise and peril of big data*, Aspen Institute, 2010.

Bracht, U., and T. Masurat, "The Digital Factory between vision and reality," *Computers in Industry* 56(4), May 2005.

Briscoe, Bob, Andrew Odlyzko, and Benjamin Tilly, *Metcalfe's law is wrong*, IEEE Spectrum, July 2006.

Brown, Robert G., and John M. Caddick, *The factory is virtual...the savings are real*, paper presented at RTO AVT symposium, 2003.

Brynjolfsson, Erik, and Adam Saunders, *Wired for innovation: How information technology is reshaping the economy* (Cambridge, MA: MIT Press, 2009).

Brynjolfsson, Erik, Lorin M. Hitt, and Heekyung Hellen Kim, *Strength in numbers: How does data-driven decisionmaking affect firm performance?*, April 22, 2011, available at SSRN (ssrn.com/abstract=1819486).

Bughin, Jacques, and Michael Chui. "The rise of the networked enterprise: Web 2.0 finds its payday," *McKinsey Quarterly*, December 2010.

Bughin, Jacques, Michael Chui, and James Manyika. "Clouds, big data, and smart assets: Ten tech-enabled trends to watch," *McKinsey Quarterly*, August 2010.

Centers for Medicare and Medicaid Services, *National Health Expenditure Projections 2009–2019,* September 2010.

Chui, Michael, Markus Löffler, and Roger Roberts, "The Internet of things," *McKinsey Quarterly*, March 2010.

Chui, Michael, Andy Miller, and Roger Roberts, "Six ways to make Web 2.0 work," *McKinsey Quarterly*, February 2009.

Congressional Budget Office, *Budget Options Volume I: Health Care,* December 2008.

Cortes, Corinna, and Vladimir Vapnik, "Support-vector networks," *Machine Learning* 20(3), September 1995.

Danker, Tony, Thomas Dohrmann, Nancy Killefer, and Lenny Mendonca, "How can American government meet its productivity challenge?" *McKinsey Quarterly*, July 2006.

Davenport, Thomas H., and Jeanne G. Harris, *Analytics at work: Smarter decisions, better results* (Cambridge, MA: Harvard Business Press, 2010).

Davenport, Thomas H., and Jeanne G. Harris, *Competing on analytics: The new science of winning* (Cambridge, MA: Harvard Business Press, 2007).

Davis, Jerel C., Laura Furstenthal, Amar A. Desai, Troy Norris, Saumya Sutaria, Edd Fleming, and Philip Ma, "The microeconomics of personalized medicine: Today's challenge and tomorrow's promise," *Nature Reviews Drug Discovery* 8, 279–286, April 2009.

Dean, Jeffrey, and Sanjay Ghemawat, *MapReduce: Simplified data processing on large clusters*, Sixth Symposium on Operating System Design and Implementation, San Francisco, CA, December 2004.

"Debunking the three leading misperceptions about health care IT," *Health International 2010*, Number 10.

(UK) Department of Health, *Usage of cancer drugs approved by NICE—review by the National Cancer Director*, September 2006.

(US) Department of Health and Human Services, *Health, United States, 2009: Special feature on medical technology*, 2009.

(US) Department of Health and Human Services, *Health, United States, 2010: Special feature on death and dying*, 2010.

Digital Forensics Association, *The leaking vault: Five years of data breaches*, July 2010.

Dohrmann, Thomas, and Lenny Mendonca, "Boosting government productivity," *McKinsey Quarterly*, November 2004.

Dohrmann, Thomas, and Gary Pinshaw, *The road to improved compliance*, McKinsey white paper, September 2009.

Drucker, Peter F., *Management challenges of the 21st century* (New York: Harper Business, 1999).

Dunleavy, P., *Innovating out of a recession*, seminar, London School of Economics, London, June 22, 2009.

Eager eyes (eagereyes.org/).

Eslami, Saied, Nicollette F. De Keizer, and Ameen Abu-Hanna, "The impact of computerized physician medication order entry in hospitalized patients: A systematic review," *International Journal of Medical Informatics*, 2008.

European Commission, *Digitizing public services in Europe: Putting ambition into action*, December 2010.

European Commission, "The 2009 ageing report: Underlying assumptions and projection methodologies," *European Economy 7*, 2008.

Farrell, Diana, Martha Laboissiere, and Jaeson Rosenfeld, "Sizing the emerging global labor market," *McKinsey Quarterly*, June 2005.

Flowing data (flowingdata.com/).

Gantz, John F., Christopher Chute, Alex Manfrediz, Stephen Minton, David Reinsel, Wolfgang Schlichting, and Anna Toncheva, "The diverse and expanding digital universe," IDC white paper, sponsored by EMC, March 2008.

Gantz, John F., and David Reinsel, "As the economy contracts, the digital universe expands," IDC white paper, sponsored by EMC, May 2009.

Gantz, John F., and David Reinsel, "The digital universe decade—Are you ready?" IDC iView, sponsored by EMC, May 2010.

Gantz, John F., David Reinsel, Christopher Chute, Wolfgang Schlichting, John McArthur, Stephen Minton, Irida Xheneti, Anna Toncheva, and Alex Manfrediz, "The expanding digital universe," IDC white paper, sponsored by EMC, March 2007.

Ghemawat, Sanjay, Howard Gobioff, and Shun-Tak Leung, *The Google file system*, 19th ACM Symposium on Operating Systems Principles, Lake George, NY, October 2003.

GigaOM on structure big data (gigaom.com/topic/structure-big-data).

Gleick, James, *The information: A history. A theory. A flood* (New York: Pantheon Books, 2011).

Goldfarb, Avi, and Catherine Tucker, *Advertising bans and the substitutability of online and offline advertising*, May 4, 2010, available at SSRN (ssrn.com/abstract=1600221).

Hajek, P., I. Havel, and M. Chytil, "The GUHA method of automatic hypotheses determination," *Computing* 1(4), 1966; 293–308.

Harding, J.A., M. Shahbaz, S. Srinivas, and A. Kusiak, "Data mining in manufacturing: A review," *Journal of Manufacturing Science and Engineering*, 2006.

Hilbert, Martin, and Priscila López, "The world's technological capacity to store, communicate, and compute information," *Science*, February 10, 2011.

Hillestad, Richard, et al., "Can electronic medical record systems transform health care? Potential health benefits, savings, and costs," *Health Affairs*, 2005.

Howe, Jeff, "The rise of crowdsourcing," *Wired*, Number 14.06, June 2006.

Hubbard, Douglas W., *How to measure anything: Finding the value of intangibles in business* (New York: Wiley, 2010).

Husted, Christian, and Nicolas Reinecke, "Improving public-sector purchasing," *McKinsey on Government*, 2009.

IBM, Collaborative User Experience Research group (www.research.ibm.com/visual/projects/history_flow/gallery.htm).

IBM, *Many eyes*, (www.958.ibm.com/software/data/cognos/manyeyes/).

Information is beautiful (www.informationisbeautiful.net/).

Jha Ashish, K., et al., "Use of electronic health records in US hospitals," *New England Journal of Medicine* 360(16), April 16, 2009:1628–1638.

Johnston, Douglas, Eric Pan, and Jan Walker, "The value of CPOE in ambulatory settings," *Journal of Healthcare Information Management*, 2004.

Jorgensen, Dale, Mun Ho, and Kevin Stiroh, "A retrospective look at the US productivity growth resurgence," *Journal of Economic Perspectives*, 2008.

Kaushal, Rainu, et al., "The costs of a national health information network," *Annals of Internal Medicine*, 2005.

Kaushik, Avinash, *Seven steps to creating a data driven decision making culture*, October 2006.

Laflamme, Francois M., Wayne E. Pietraszek, and Nilesh V. Rajadhyax, "Reforming hospitals with IT investment," *McKinsey Quarterly*, August 2010.

Lohr, Steve, "For today's graduate, just one word: Statistics," *New York Times*, August 5, 2009.

Lonti, Z., and M. Woods, *Towards government at a glance: Identification of core data and issues related to public sector efficiency*, OECD Working Papers on Public Governance, No. 7, OECD Publishing, doi:10.1787/245570167540.

Lyman, Peter, and Hal Varian, *How much information? 2003, School of Information Management and Systems,* University of California at Berkeley, 2003.

Magoulas, Roger, and Ben Lorica, "Big data: Technologies and techniques for large scale data," *Release 2.0*, Number 11, February 2009.

Mango, Paul D., and Vivian E. Riefberg, "Three imperatives for improving US health care," *McKinsey Quarterly*, December 2008.

McKinsey & Company for IAB Europe, *Consumers driving the digital uptake: The economic value of online advertising-based services for consumers*, September 2010.

McKinsey Global Institute, *Accounting for the cost of US health care: A new look at why Americans spend more*, December 2008.

McKinsey Global Institute, *Beyond austerity: A path to economic growth and renewal in Europe*, October 2010.

McKinsey Global Institute, *Changing the fortunes of America's workforce: A human capital challenge*, June 2009.

McKinsey Global Institute, *Debt and deleveraging: The global credit bubble and its economic consequences*, January 2010.

McKinsey Global Institute, *From austerity to prosperity: Seven priorities for the long term*, November 2010.

McKinsey Global Institute, *Growth and competitiveness in the United States: The role of its multinational companies*, June 2010.

McKinsey Global Institute, *Growth and renewal in the United States: Retooling America's economic engine*, February 2011.

McKinsey Global Institute, *How IT enables productivity growth*, October 2002.

McKinsey Global Institute, *US productivity growth, 1995–2000,* October 2001.

Mekhjian, Hagop S., et. al., "Immediate benefits realized following implementation of physician order entry at an academic medical center," *Journal of the American Medical Informatics Association*, 9:529–539, 2002.

Miller, George A., "The magical number seven, plus or minus two: Some limits on our capacity for processing information," *Psychological Review*, Volume 63(2), March 1956: 81–97.

MIT Senseable City Laboratory (senseable.mit.edu/).

National Center for Health Statistics, Centers for Disease Control and Prevention, *Electronic medical record/electronic health record use by office-based physicians*, December 2009.

Nature on big data (www.nature.com/news/specials/bigdata/index.html)

OECD, *Monitoring taxpayers' compliance: A practical guide based on revenue body experience*, June 2008.

Oliner, Stephen, and Daniel Sichel, "Information technology and productivity: Where we are now and where we are going?", Federal Reserve Bank of Atlanta *Economic Review*, 2002.

O'Reilly Radar on data coverage and insight (radar.oreilly.com/data/).

Pearson, Mark, OECD Health Division, *Written statement to Senate Special Committee on Aging*, September 2009.

Peterson, Chris L., and Rachel Burton, *US health care spending: Comparison with other OECD countries*, Congressional Research Service, September 2007.

Ponemon Institute, *Fourth annual US cost of data breach study*, January 2009.

Potts, Amy L., Frederick E. Barr, David F. Gregory, Lorianne Wright, and Neal R. Patel, "Computerized physician order entry and medication errors in a pediatric critical care unit," *Pediatrics* 113(1), 2004:59–63.

PwC Health Industries, *The price of excess: Identifying waste in healthcare spending*, 2009.

Shapiro, Carl, and Hal R. Varian, *Information Rules: A strategic guide to the network economy* (Cambridge, MA: Harvard Business Press, 1998).

Schonlau, Matthias, "The clustergram: A graph for visualizing hierarchical and non hierarchical cluster analyses," *The Stata Journal*, 2002; 2 (4): 391–402.

Simon, Herbert A., "Designing organizations for an information-rich world," in Martin Greenberger, *Computers, communication, and the public interest* (Baltimore, MD: The Johns Hopkins Press, 1971).

"A special report: Dealing with data," *Science*, February 11, 2011.

"A special report on managing information: Data, data everywhere," *The Economist*, February 25, 2010.

The Technium (www.kk.org/thetechnium/)

Think Quarterly (thinkquarterly.co.uk/).

Thomke, Stefan H., *Experimentation matters: Unlocking the potential of new technologies for innovation* (Cambridge, MA: Harvard Business Press, 2003).

Varian, Hal. *Computer mediated transactions*, 2010 Ely Lecture at the American Economics Association meeting, Atlanta, Georgia.

Viegas, Fernanda B., Martin Wattenberg, and Kushal Dave, *Studying cooperation and conflict between authors with history flow visualizations,* CHI2004 proceedings of the SIGCHI conference on human factors in computing systems, 2004.

Walker, Jan, et al., "The value of health care information exchange and interoperability," *Health Affairs*, 2005.

Wikipedia (http://en.wikipedia.org/).

Yankee Group, *Global mobile forecast*, December 2010.

Relevant McKinsey Global Institute publications

August 2010
Clouds, big data, and smart assets:
Ten tech-enabled business trends to watch

Advancing technologies and their swift adoption are upending traditional business models. Senior executives need to think strategically about how to prepare their organizations for the challenging new environment.

March 2010
The Internet of Things

More objects are becoming embedded with sensors and gaining the ability to communicate. The resulting new information networks promise to create new business models, improve business processes, and reduce costs and risks.

December 2008
Accounting for the cost of US health care:
A new look at why Americans spend more

The United States spends $650 billion more on health care than expected, even when adjusting for the economy's relative wealth; MGI examines the underlying trends and key drivers of these higher costs. MGI finds that outpatient care, which includes same-day hospital and physician office visits, is by far the largest and fastest-growing part of the US health system. The next largest contributors are the cost of drugs, and administration and insurance.

October 2002
How IT enables productivity growth

Looking at three sectors in detail—retail banking, retail trade, and semiconductors—MGI finds that while IT enabled productivity gains in each sector, its impact was complex and varied. IT applications that had a high impact on productivity shared three characteristics: They were tailored to sector-specific business processes and linked to performance levers; they were deployed in a sequence that allowed companies to leverage their previous IT investments effectively; and they evolved in conjunction with managerial innovation.

October 2001
US productivity growth 1995–2000: Understanding the contributions of information technology relative to other factors

MGI's study of US productivity growth aimed to determine the causes of the sudden increase in the growth rate of labor productivity in the United States between 1995 and 2000. This increase was interpreted by key economists and policy makers as evidence of a "new economy," where IT applications would lead to faster US economic growth. The report lays out the nature and importance of the role played by six key sectors in the acceleration of productivity growth and its causes, with a focus on the role of IT.

www.mckinsey.com/mgi

eBook versions of selected MGI reports are available on MGI's Web site, on Amazon's Kindle bookstore, and on Apple's iBookstore.

Download and listen to MGI podcasts on iTunes or at
www.mckinsey.com/mgi/publications/

Made in the USA
Lexington, KY
02 October 2013